MITTENS FROM AROUND NORWAY

NINA GRANLUND SÆTHER

MITTENS FROM AROUND NORWAY

Over 40 Traditional Knitting Patterns

INSPIRED BY FOLK ART
COLLECTIONS

TRAFALGAR SQUARE
North Pomfret, Vermont

First published in the United States of America
in 2017 by
Trafalgar Square Books
North Pomfret, Vermont 05053

Originally published in Norwegian as *Strikkemønstre
fra hele Norge.*

Copyright © 2016 Cappelen Damm AS
English translation © 2017 Trafalgar Square Books

The author received support from the Norwegian
Non-fiction Writers and Translators Organization.

ISBN: 978-1-57076-822-4

Library of Congress Control Number: 2017931403

PHOTOGRAPHY: Guri Pfeifer; for exceptions, see page 191.
CHARTS AND ILLUSTRATIONS: Nina Granlund Sæther
BOOK DESIGN: Sissel Holt Boniface
TRANSLATOR: Carol Huebscher Rhoades

Printed in China

10 9 8 7 6 5 4 3 2

CONTENTS

Why a book about mittens?

In a country where it's easy to end up with cold fingers more than six months of the year, mittens are an important piece of clothing! Throughout history, Norwegians have had to protect themselves to avoid freezing. For that reason, we have a long and rich tradition of making mittens with a variety of techniques.

Both a *nålbound* (needle-woven) wool mitten and several leather mittens found in excavations in Oslo and Trondheim have been dated to the Middle Ages, but there are very few truly old mittens preserved here or in the other Nordic countries. We also haven't found much in written sources from before the 1700s. The oldest Norwegian knitted mittens we can date with certainty are from 1772—a well-preserved pair from Røros with a shag fringe and decorative sewing on the back of the hand. One mitten is embroidered with the initials OISR and the other with the year.

It's likely that these mittens were knitted by Johanna Jonsdatter (who was born in 1747) and that the mittens were a so-called "lover's gift." This pair is noted in the registry of the Røros Museum, knitted in stockinette with blue wool yarn and embroidered with chain stitch.

Johanna was engaged to Ole Jensen Røraas on May 3rd, 1772, and they were married a month and a half later, on June 21st, 1772. This information was recorded in the church registry for Røros.

The letters on the mittens, OISR, indicate precisely to whom the mittens belonged— Ole IensSøn Røraas (1732-1804). There aren't any extant records of anyone else in the Røros area with initials that match.

In the old days, mittens were a typical engagement gift, and girls became especially proficient at that type of knitting, making their mittens as pretty as they could. This pair of mittens was made particularly carefully—with lovely embroidery in gold, green, and red, and a decorative fringe on the edges in the same colors. There are small green tassels at each side.

There isn't very much information about this married pair, but we know they lived in Maglivold, because that's where they appear in the national census for Røros from 1801. Ole was a "tenant farmer and miner." They had a daughter aged 18 and a 23-year-old son when they lived there. They also had a servant girl. In addition, Johanna's sister and her husband (also a miner) lived there as lodgers.

Knitted textiles are seldom mentioned in writing. However, in the estate distribution of Malena Pedersdatter Kuraasen, who died in Røros in 1782, we find mentioned "1 pair torn blue mittens and 1 green knitted sweater." From Peder Hiort's will in 1788, we learn that women in Røros were familiar with knitting. So it's not inconceivable that blue mittens of this type were relatively common in that area of Norway at the end of the eighteenth century.

The ingeniously easy technique of knitting is surprisingly young, but we don't know much about its origins. The oldest knitted textiles ever discovered were found in Egypt, dating from around 1000 CE. These com-

The year 1772 is embroidered on these knitted wedding mittens from Røros.
They are the oldest extant example of Norwegian knitted mittens.

plex and colorful fragments of pattern-knit stockings demonstrate that the technique was already well developed by then.

Two knitted pillow covers in silk, which were found in a royal Spanish grave, are the earliest example of European knitted work. The pillow covers have been dated to about 1275. Both preserved examples and written sources indicate that the standards of handwork guilds were very high by the thirteenth and fourteenth centuries. A series of paintings of the Virgin Mary with a knitted garment in her hands show that it was common to knit in the round with 4 or 5 needles. By this time, knitting was well established in northern Italy and Germany.

The technique of knitting reached England and Scotland by the 1400s, and under Elizabeth I it spread widely. Knitting schools were opened to help the poor. That might

have inspired Christian IV (king of Denmark and Norway) to do something similar when he came to power.

Nevertheless, there are very few preserved examples of knitted garments that would have been made before 1600. The Museum of London has a children's mitten from the 1500s in its collections. This mitten has a simple contrast-color band around the wrist. The Victoria and Albert Museum in London has a pair of Spanish gloves made with red silk yarn and silver gilt thread, also from the 1500s. The gloves, which belonged to a bishop, are decorated with religious symbols.

They were knitted with yarn almost as fine as sewing thread, because the gauge is approximately 92 stitches in 4 inches / 10 centimeters. Gilt thread was laid in around the fingers to give the impression that the

The technique of knitting is relatively young. Nevertheless, it was already well developed in central Europe in the Middle Ages. These Spanish gloves, in the collections of the Victoria and Albert Museum in London, were made with silk yarn and silver gilt thread in the 1500s. The gauge is approximately 92 stitches in 4 inches / 10 centimeters.

glove was sewn out of leather. The thumb was knitted separately and sewn on.

This type of work was knitted by professionals—that is, men. In a number of countries, knitting was organized and handled by guilds, in the same way as other artisanal activities. Their customers were the royal house, church, and nobility. Guilds ensured that craftsmen studied their trades for a certain amount of time, and progressed from apprentice to journeyman and then master. They also used their power to regulate who could be admitted to the profession and to stop competition.

Professional secrets were protected, of course. But knitting spread anyway, like fire in dry grass. It was well established in Iceland and the Faroe Islands in the sixteenth century, and had likely also reached Denmark and Sweden.

During restoration work on Bryggen in Bergen, they found a knitted fragment from the sixteenth century, but we don't know whether the garment was made in Norway or imported. So far, there are no other traces of knitted goods in Norway before 1566 and 1567. That find was a pair of old and torn stockings made in the Faroe Islands and recorded making their way to Bergenhus. (They were confiscated from the home of a man who was executed.)

Some sources indicate that the technique of knitting was known in Rogaland and Trøndelag in the 1630s. Wherever it began, during the seventeenth and eighteenth centuries, knitting spread to almost every part of Norway.

There are very few Norwegian knitted garments from the eighteenth century. Two pairs of mittens from 1787, as well as the previously described mittens from Røros, are the exceptions rather than the rule.

Both of the 1787 pairs are embellished with embroidery and have colorful fringes on the cuffs. One pair is knitted using two-end knitting and comes from Lærdal in Sogn. This pair can be seen in the Norwegian collection of the Nordic Museum in Stockholm. The other pair, of unknown origin, belongs to the Norwegian Folk Museum.

Norway has been known for its knitted Selbu mittens for a long time. By 1883, two pairs of mittens were sent to a large exhibition in Kristiania (now Oslo), and since 1897, mittens from Selbu have been sold in other places: first at the Friends of Norwegian Handcraft center in Trondheim and then all around the country. After World War I, sales of Selbu mittens exploded. Mitten knitting became an important home industry at a time when it was difficult to find other income. In the 1930s, production was enormous, and in 1937 more than 90,000 pairs of mittens were exported from the little town of Selbu to the U.S. and to

winter sports centers in southern Europe. In Norway, Selbu mittens became high fashion, and Selbu knitting was a natural part of the Norwegian athletes' Olympic uniforms for many years. Selbu mittens became a national symbol. Even though mittens and gloves are available in all types of modern fibers these days, knitted wool mittens still have pride of place in Norway. There's scarcely a home in the country where you can't find at least one pair of black and white pattern-knitted mittens.

Of course, every pair of mittens knitted with two colors isn't necessarily from Selbu, even if they have some of the same hallmarks! With this book, I wanted to explore traditions from other parts of Norway, and showcase some of the many textile treasures that are not as well known. I've also included some of my own mitten designs.

Ever since Ingebjørg Gravjord published her book *Mittens in the Norwegian Tradition* in 1986, I've had a love for Norwegian

By the 1500s, knitting had reached Iceland and the Faroe Islands. It's likely that it also reached Denmark and Sweden relatively early on. This glove, from the collection of the Nordic Museum in Stockholm, was pattern-knit with two colors and has the date (1800) knitted in.

mittens. Ingebjørg examined all sorts of mittens and placed them in a European costume context. The book was a pioneer work, and together with Knitting in Norway—which she was also involved in making—is one of the most important textile histories in Norway. I was lucky enough to have Ingebjørg as my instructor in textile history at the State's Teacher's School in design in Oslo in the early 1980s, and I also met with her on several occasions when I worked as a journalist and editor at Norwegian Handcrafts. We had all kinds of interesting conversations about Norwegian knitting traditions, and her work has inspired me in so many ways.

Textiles are perishable. Mittens that are used soon become worn out. A darned and repaired mitten isn't as strong as one that's new and whole. Many mittens were originally made for festivals and church days, and, over time, were demoted to everyday mittens. When they could no longer be repaired, they were thrown out or sent to a shoddy mill. There, the wool could be carded and spun into new yarn, or recycled as filling. For those reasons, there are relatively few mittens preserved. Some treasures have been saved, however.

Many of these objects can be viewed today via Digitalmuseum.no, which catalogues both garments in museum collections and garments that are privately owned. Many were registered in connection with the large traveling exhibition "Knitting then and now" in 1983-84, which was a collaboration between Norway's Handcraft Association and the Norwegian Folk Museum. Still, not everything has been digitalized. Many of the pictures you'll find there are not high quality. With a generous project grant from the Norwegian Publisher's Association for authors and translators, I had the opportunity to visit a number of museums around the country and look at their collections. This was fantastically fun, and there's a big difference between looking at a small, low-resolution photo on a screen and getting permission to see the textiles in person.

I've also tried to immerse myself in the written history of European knitting traditions, especially when it comes to Norwegian mittens. I have, among other things, greatly benefited from finding old instruction books about handcrafts.

Among these, I must name Heidi Fossnes's book, *Håndplagg til bunader og folkedrakter* [Handcoverings for national and folk costumes], published in 2003. It's been an important source of information and shows the diversity to be found in mittens, gloves, and other garments for the hands from all around Norway.

Finally, I'd like to mention that the mittens you'll find patterns for in this book are not necessarily exact copies of their traditional inspiration. Modern yarn is different, and I've chosen to indulge myself with more colors. I've also adapted the mittens to be more suitable for our era.

Asker, August 2015

Nina Granlund Sæther on the internet: ww.hjertebank.no
Facebook: Hjertebank Nina Granlund Sæther

10

Selbu mittens are well known outside Norway's borders. The small town in South Trøndelag has a fantastic mitten tradition which is still very much alive. Everything knitted in black and white is not, however, Selbu knitting. With this book, I've tried to showcase other less well-known mitten designs, from Halden and Kristiansand in the south to Kautokeino in the north. All of Norway's regions are represented—in addition to a selection of my own mitten designs.

BEFORE YOU BEGIN: GOOD TIPS

Gauge (Tension): To ensure the finished garment will be the expected size, it's important that the gauge be accurate. If you knit loosely, the mittens will be too big. In that case, choose smaller needles. Conversely, if you knit too tightly, the mittens will be too small, so choose larger needles.

Sizes: Most of the mittens here are given in two sizes. The chart is the same for each size; sizing is adjusted by changing the gauge.

Charts: All the charts are read from right to left and from the bottom up. At the side of each chart, you'll find a key explaining the various symbols and colors. Where there are no squares, there are no stitches. If there's an open space in the chart, follow the line of the chart to the next square/stitch. When the number of stitches in the thumb gusset increases in width, you must add a stitch.

Unless otherwise specified in the pattern with a dot where this should occur, increase a new stitch where shown in the drawing. When the number of stitches at the top decreases, it means you should decrease.

Shaping by Decreasing on the Right Side:
Slip 1 st, knit 1, pass slipped st over (or work ssk: slip 1 knitwise, slip 1 knitwise; insert left needle tip into sts left to right and knit the sts together).

Shaping by Decreasing on the Left Side: Knit 2 sts together.

Stranded Color Knitting: When knitting in pattern with two or more colors, it's important that the strands don't change places on the wrong side. If you switch the position of the colors as you work, you will soon see the error. This is called "color dominance"; changing the positions of the colors will affect which one is dominant.

Floating Strands on WS: It's not a good idea to leave long strands on the wrong side—your fingers can get caught in the yarn! In these patterns, when there are more than 6-7 stitches in one color, I recommend that you twist the strands around each other on the wrong side.

ABBREVIATIONS

BO	bind off (= British cast off)
cm	centimeter(s)
CO	cast on
dec	decrease
dpn	double-pointed needles
in	inch(es)
inc	increase
k	knit
k2tog	knit 2 sts together = 1 st decreased
M1	make 1 – lift strand between 2 sts and knit into back loop
m	meter(s)
mm	millimeters
p	purl
psso	pass slipped stitch over
rem	remain(ing)(s)
rep	repeat
rnd(s)	round(s)
RS	right side
sl	slip
ssk	slip, slip, knit = (sl 1 knitwise) 2 times, knit the 2 sts together through back loops

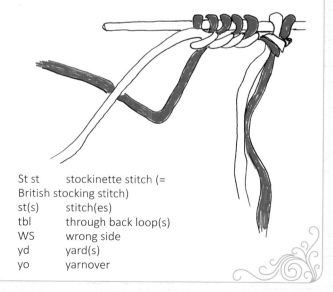

St st	stockinette stitch (= British stocking stitch)
st(s)	stitch(es)
tbl	through back loop(s)
WS	wrong side
yd	yard(s)
yo	yarnover

Avoid twisting the yarns in the same place every time around, however, as the stacked strands will show through on the right side.

Needles: All the mittens in this book are knitted in the round on 5 double-pointed needles, unless otherwise specified.

Casting On: Some of the designs begin with a two-color cast-on. Begin with a slip knot of both colors held together and then continue with one strand of each color. One color forms the loops on the needle and the other the diagonals below (see drawing). When you begin knitting, remove the slip knot.

Two-End Knitting:
In several patterns, there are one or more rows of two-end knitting (also called twined knitting or purl braiding). The technique prevents the edge from rolling up, and is worked with both yarns held in front of the work.

The purl braid is worked with two strands of the same color or two different colors—for example, 1 red and 1 white, as illustrated here.

Bring both yarns to the front of the work.

Bring the red to the right over the white and purl a stitch with white. Leaving the white on the front, hold it to the right over the red.

Purl one stitch with red. Leaving the red on the front, hold it to the right over the white.

Continue the same way around. The yarn you work with next will always be under the one you just knitted with.

As you purl around, the strands will twist around each other—you'll need to untwist them occasionally.

Usually one round of purl braid is enough to keep the edge from rolling up.

You can also repeat this round or work with the yarns twisted in the opposite direction. The yarn you just knitted with will lie under, not over, the other strand. The diagonal lines will mirror each other and form chevrons, and the twisting of the previous round will be undone.

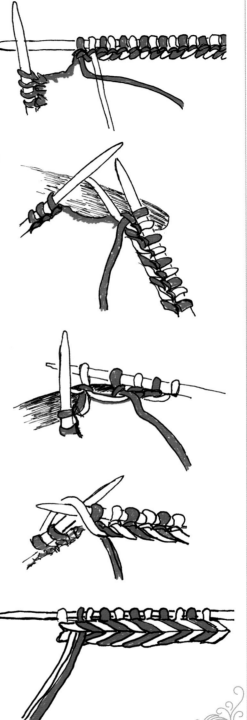

Turn the mitten upside down and follow the same procedure for the stitches above the waste yarn. Begin 1 stitch to the right of the waste yarn. Continue, picking up the right leg of each stitch until you have the specified number of stitches on the needle.

Carefully remove the waste yarn and divide the stitches onto 4 needles.

Thumb

When the instructions say, "Set aside 15 sts for the thumb," it's easiest to knit those 15 sts with smooth waste yarn in a contrast color. Slip the stitches back to the left needle and knit them with the working yarn (either single color or as shown on the chart).

When the rest of the mitten is finished, pick up the stitches below and above the waste yarn using a double-pointed needle. (For example, the pattern might say, "pick up 17 + 17 sts for the thumb.") Use a double-pointed needle to pick up the stitches below the waste yarn. To avoid holes, always begin 1 stitch to the right before the waste yarn. Slide the needle from right to left, picking up the right leg of each stitch. Continue across until you have the specified number of stitches.

In some of the patterns in this book, the stitch counts below and above the thumbhole don't match. In that case, don't use the waste yarn method for setting aside stitches. Instead, slip the thumb stitches onto a safety pin, a length of yarn, or a yarn holder. On the next round, cast on the specified number of stitches.

Mittens from Idd

We don't know when people began knitting patterns with two colors here in Norway. Most likely, this idea appeared at the beginning of the 1800s, and could have come from Shetland and the Faroe Islands to the west, Denmark and the Netherlands in the south, or Sweden and Finland to the east. We have several preserved sweaters from the middle of the nineteenth century. The oldest one has a very advanced design—in other words, not a beginner's project. It's from Stord, and has the year 1846 knitted in.

A pair of mittens from the neighborhood of Ør in Idd—now Halden—has the date of 1858 knitted in on one cuff. They are the oldest patterned mittens we can date with certainty. The other cuff features the initials LOS.

As early as the 1790s, General-Major and topographer Engelbrecht Hansen Hoff (1739-1811) described women knitting in Idd:

"The women here are, in general, more hardworking and cleverer than the men; as they go about their household duties, they occupy themselves with spinning, weaving, sewing, and knitting stockings, yes, it isn't uncommon to see them out on their errands, walking on the path and knitting stockings or mittens…"

These mittens have a simple block pattern in black and green repeated around the mitten. I decided to make the folded cuff a little longer than on the original and omitted the date and initials.

The initials LOS are knitted in on the cuff of one mitten and the date, 1858, is on the other.

Thumb

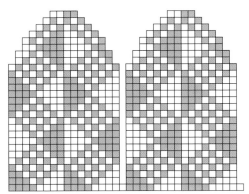

☒ Gray—knit
☐ Green—knit

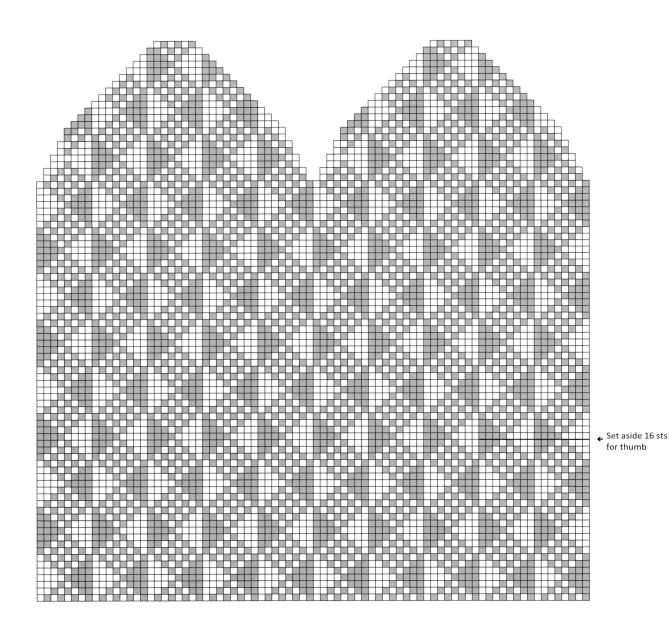

← Set aside 16 sts for thumb

INSTRUCTIONS

Sizes: Women's (Men's)

MATERIALS
Yarn:
CYCA #1 (fingering) 2-ply Gammelserie from Rauma (100% wool, 175 yd/160 m / 50 g), Gray 405: 50 (100) g
Løyegarn (embroidery yarn) from Setesdal Handcraft, Green 50 (100) g
OR substitute Dale Baby Ull [CYCA #1 (fingering), 100% wool (180 yd/165 m / 50 g)], Light Olive 2231

Needles: U.S. size 0 (1.5) / 2 (2.5) mm, set of 5 dpn

Gauge: 36 (33) sts = 4 in / 10 cm.
Adjust needle size to obtain correct gauge if necessary.

Right Mitten
With Gray, CO 81 sts. Divide sts onto 4 dpn and join, being careful not to twist cast-on row. Work around in k2, p2 ribbing for 3½ in / 9 cm. Dec 1 st to 80 sts and continue in St st following the chart. At the dark line, set aside 16 sts for thumb (see page 15 for details). Shape top of mitten as shown on the chart (see page 13 for details). Cut yarn and draw end through rem sts; tighten.

Thumb
Pick up 17 + 17 sts = total of 34 sts (see page 15). Divide sts onto 4 dpn and work as shown on thumb chart. Cut yarn and draw end through rem sts; tighten.

Left Mitten
Work as for right mitten, reversing thumb placement.

Finishing
Weave in all ends neatly on WS. Gently steam press under a damp pressing cloth to block. Fold cuff up to double.

Mittens from Asker

On a winter's day early in March 1940, photographer Anders Beer Wilse took a series of photos of a young Prince Harald on Skaugum. Our future king had just turned three years old. The little prince was photographed skiing, on a kick sled, with a toboggan, and together with a snowman—dressed in stretch pants and ski boots, a red sweater with white patterning, and ditto for the cap and red mittens. No one knows who knitted this fine outfit.

Just a few days after Prince Harald turned three, on February 21st, 1940, he was photographed out in the snow at Skaugum. The knitted sweater has been saved so we know that the outfit was all red and white. The prince wore the same outfit when the royal family fled Norway on the night of April 9, to escape the German invasion.

I also grew up in Asker. The mittens the prince wore are very similar to the first pair of mittens I knitted—the only difference is that the cuffs on the prince's mittens were knitted with k1, p1 ribbing instead of k2, p2.

I was a student at the Heggedal elementary school in Asker, and in the third or fourth grade, we had to sew a gym bag and knit mittens. That must have been in the fall of 1969 or 1970.

My first pair of mittens was turquoise, knitted with Alpe yarn from Hovland Mill. The yarn came in 50 g balls, in contrast to other yarns in skeins that had to be wound into balls.

Thumb

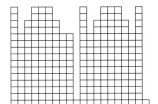

☐ Knit
ⓥ Purl

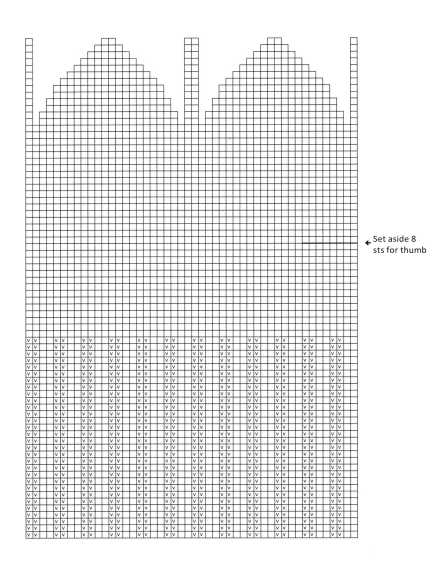

← Set aside 8
sts for thumb

INSTRUCTIONS

This is an easy pattern that can be adjusted for several sizes.

Sizes: 4 (6, 8) years

MATERIALS
Yarn:
CYCA #2 (sport), PT5 from Rauma (80% wool, 20% nylon, 140 yd/128 m / 50 g), Turquoise 571: 50 (50, 50) g

Needles: U.S. size 1.5 (2.5, 4) / 2.5 (3, 3.5) mm, set of 5 dpn

Gauge: 29 (28, 27) sts = 4 in / 10 cm.
Adjust needle size to obtain correct gauge if necessary.

Right Mitten
CO 48 sts. Divide sts onto 4 dpn and join, being careful not to twist cast-on row. Work around in k2, p2 ribbing for 3¼ in / 8 cm. Continue in St st following the chart. At the dark line, work 8 sts with smooth waste yarn, slide sts back to left needle, and knit with working yarn (see page 15 for details). Work until the piece covers the little finger. Shape top of mitten as shown on the chart and following details below.

Top Shaping
Make sure you have 12 sts on each needle.
** *K1, ssk. Knit until 2 sts rem on 2nd dpn. K2tog, k1*. Rep * to * over the next two dpn. Knit 1 rnd without decreasing**.
Rep ** to ** a total of 3 times.
Now decrease on every rnd (that is, from * to *). When 2 sts rem on each dpn, cut yarn and draw end through rem sts; tighten.

Thumb
Pick up 10 + 10 sts = total of 20 sts (see page 15. Divide the sts onto 4 dpn and knit around in St st. After the 1st rnd, k2tog at each side to eliminate any holes = 18 sts total rem. Continue around to the tip of the thumb. Shape tip as for top of mitten, working ** to ** twice. Cut yarn and draw end through rem sts; tighten.

Left Mitten
Work as for right mitten, reversing thumb placement.

Finishing
Weave in all ends neatly on WS. Gently steam press under a damp pressing cloth to block.

Snowflakes

Spinning wool, cotton, or linen yarn takes both time and labor. When the textile industry was mechanized in England at the end of the 1700s, efficiency increased enormously. Norway had considerable amounts of water power and, by 1815, we already had a cotton mill in Halden. It wasn't until the middle of the 1800s, though, that the industry really took off. The Dale mill saw the light of day in 1879; Sandnes Uldvarefabrik in 1888, Hillesvåg Ullvarefabrikk in 1898; and Rauma Ullvarefabrikk wasn't established until 1927.

Aalgaard's Woolen Mill in Rogaland, which was founded in 1870, was the first mill in Norway to begin custom spinning. The farmers brought in wool and got yarn back. Wool products contributed an important supplementary income for many and, with yarn from the mill, women in the district could weave much more.

Yarn spun for knitting was not regularly available on the market until some years later. Dale Yarn in Vaksdal, for example, began producing knitting yarn in 1912. Commercially-spun yarn was expensive and so handspun was more commonly used until the period between the world wars.

All sorts of stars have been widely used as motifs in Norwegian knitted textiles. The stars featured on the palms of these mittens are often knitted in Selbu and are locally called "spit balls." Many Norwegian designers have used snowflakes in their designs and I wanted to make my own snowflakes. I fell headlong in love with the blue yarn that was used when I came upon it in New York. With this motif, it's easy to enjoy the fine color nuances of the yarn.

The spinning wheel became common in Norway in the 1700s. It quickly became one of the most important work tools. The woman in the photo is carding wool. Varaldsøy, 1869-70.

Thumb

☐ White—knit
▨ Blue—knit
⊻ Blue—purl

← Set aside 17 sts
for thumb

INSTRUCTIONS

Sizes: Women's (Men's)

MATERIALS
Yarn:
CYCA #1 (fingering), Dale Baby Ull (100% wool, 180 yd/165 m / 50 g), White 0017: 50 (100) g
CYCA #2 (sport), Arroyo from Malabrigo (100% Merino wool, 335 yd/306 m / 100 g), Azules 856: 50 (100) g OR substitute Dale Baby Ull, Blue 5545

Needles: U.S. size 1.5 (2.5) / 2.5 (3) mm, set of 5 dpn

Gauge: 32 (29) sts = 4 in / 10 cm.
Adjust needle size to obtain correct gauge if necessary.

Right Mitten
With Blue, CO 62 sts. Divide sts onto 4 dpn and join, being careful not to twist cast-on row. Work around in k1, p1 ribbing for the first rnd, as shown on the chart. Purl the next rnd. Now continue in St st following the chart. Increase for the thumb gusset as indicated on the chart until there are 17 sts for the thumb. Place the 17 sts on a holder and CO 16 sts over the gap. Continue the pattern and shape the top as shown on the chart (see page 13 for details). Cut yarn and draw end through rem sts; tighten.

Thumb
Pick up 19 + 19 sts around the thumbhole = 38 sts total. Divide sts onto 4 dpn and work as shown on thumb chart. Cut yarn and draw end through rem sts; tighten.

Left Mitten
Work mirror-image from chart.

Finishing
Weave in all ends neatly on WS. Gently steam press under a damp pressing cloth to block.

Caroline Halvorsen's Mittens

In 1847, Denmark published its first knitting book. It was a few more years before a similar book was published in Norway. There were some knitting patterns in Marie Blom's book *Household Help and Patterns for the Instruction of Everyone*, published in 1888. The patterns included "Knee Socks" for gout patients and the "Crown Princess's Trondheim Skirt." There weren't any mitten patterns, but "Good Gloves for Men and Women" were featured in the book.

In 1901, Caroline Halvorsen's *Knitting Book for Schools and Home* came out. For the first time, Norwegians had an educational book which explained the ground rules of knitting techniques, from the simplest little swatch to advanced stockings, skirts, and bed coverings. With the help of the text, photos, and drawings, Halvorsen (1853-1926) explained how students should learn to knit, year by year.

Halvorsen was among the first students at The Women's Industry School in Kristiania when it opened in 1875. The following year, she was hired as a teacher. All the way until 1923, she was the leader of the handcraft teachers' education program in Norway. She had been given a solid foundational knowledge of knitting, sewing, and weaving by her mother.

Halvorsen wrote a series of books about the various handcrafts. Her knitting book was the basis for all knitting instruction in Norwegian schools until the 1950s and '60s. Several mitten patterns in these books explain why so many museums in Norway have the same mittens in their collections.

Mittens embellished with cables and fans were usually called bride's mittens or church mittens, and, eventually, Sunday mittens. There might be a cable in the center and lace fan patterns on each side or lacy fans in the center and cables on the sides. Caroline Halvorsen didn't write complete instructions for the mittens but described how to make the cables and fans and suggested that one could make mittens, coverlets, and similar items with the pattern. This is my variation.

In Johanna Schreiner's book, *Knitting Patterns from Great-Grandmother's Time*, which came out a few years later, there's a pattern with a combination of cables and fans. So it's no surprise that this type of mitten is recognized in many corners of Norway.

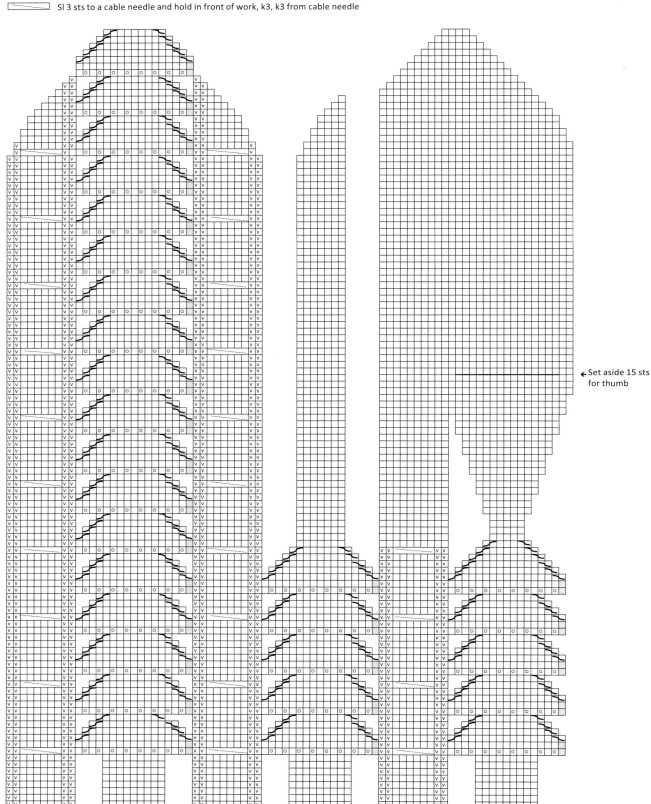

← Set aside 15 sts for thumb

Thumb

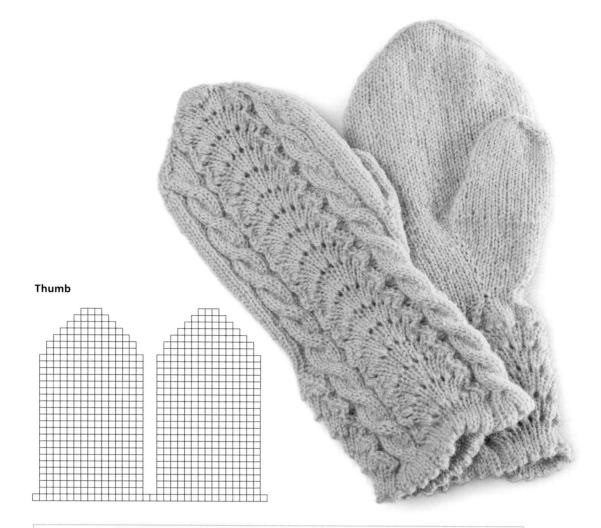

INSTRUCTIONS

Sizes: Women's

MATERIALS

Yarn:
CYCA #2 (sport), Ask (Hifa 2) from Hillesvåg Ullvarefabrikk (100% wool, 345 yd/315 m / 100 g), Golden Yellow 6094: 100 g

Needles: U.S. size 1.5 / 2.5 mm, set of 5 dpn

Gauge: 26 sts = 4 in / 10 cm.
Adjust needle size to obtain correct gauge if necessary.

Right Mitten
CO 57 sts and divide sts over dpn. Join to work in the round. Knit around in St st for ¾ in / 2 cm. Make an eyelet rnd: (k2tog, yo) around. Now work following the chart, increasing as shown. At dark line on chart, set aside 15 sts for thumbhole (see page 15

for details). Above the thumbhole, work the palm in St st and the back of the hand in lace and cable pattern as on the chart. Shape the top as indicated on the chart (see page 13 for details). Cut yarn and draw end through rem sts; tighten.

Thumb
Pick up and knit 17 + 17 sts around thumbhole = 34 sts total (see page 15). Divide sts onto 4 dpn and work as shown on thumb chart. Cut yarn and draw end through rem sts; tighten.

Left Mitten
Work mirror-image from chart.

Finishing
Weave in all ends neatly on WS. Gently steam press under a damp pressing cloth to block.

Rose Mittens from Oslo

In its collection, the Norwegian Folk Museum has a pair of distinctive mittens with an all-over flower pattern. The information about these men's mittens is sparse and it's not at all certain that they originated in Norway's capital. When people first collected items for museums, it was the items themselves that were the point, not the use or user.

The mittens were knitted on fine needles with black and white wool yarn. The museum also has a pair with black roses on a white background.

Rounding the corners of an eight-petaled rose stylizes the flowers. You can find similar roses on many different knitted garments. Here, the roses are closely spaced to cover the entire mitten.

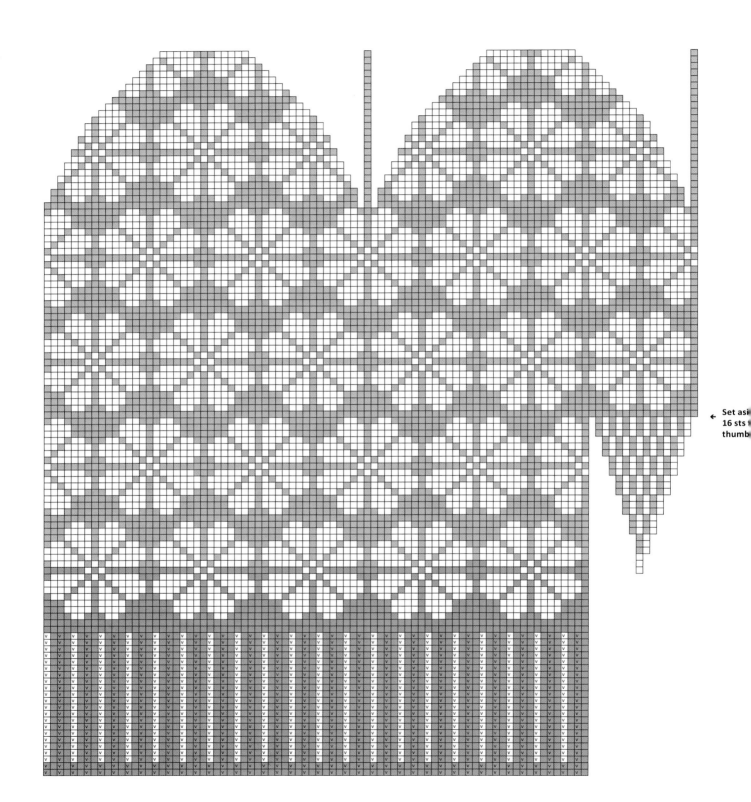

Set asi
16 sts
thumb

White—knit
☑ White—purl
▨ Gray—knit
▨ Gray—purl

Thumb

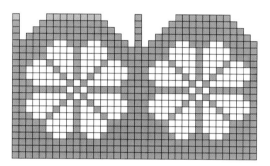

INSTRUCTIONS

Sizes: Women's (Men's)

MATERIALS
Yarn:
CYCA #2 (sport), Fine 2-ply Old Spelsau wool yarn from Selbu Spinneri (can be substituted with Ask / Hifa 2 from Hillesvåg) (100% wool, 345 yd/315 m / 100 g), White: 100 (100) g
CYCA #1 (fingering), Fine 2-ply Trøndersau yarn from Selbu Spinneri (100% wool, 345 yd/315 m / 100 g), Natural Gray: 100 (100) g

Needles: U.S. size 000 (0) / 1.5 (2) mm, set of 5 dpn

Gauge: 40 (36) sts = 4 in / 10 cm.
Adjust needle size to obtain correct gauge if necessary.

Right Mitten
With Gray, CO 80 sts and divide sts evenly over 4 dpn. Join to work in the round. Work around in k1, p1 ribbing as shown on the chart. After the first two rnds in Gray, add White. Work (3 sts Gray, 1 st White)

as shown on chart; the center Gray st and all the White sts are purled. After ribbing is complete, change to St st and continue following the pattern. Increase as shown for the thumb gusset. At the dark line, set aside 16 sts for the thumb (see page 15 for details). Continue, shaping top of mitten as shown on chart (see page 13 for details). Cut yarn and draw end through rem sts; tighten.

Thumb
Pick up and knit 18 + 18 sts around thumbhole = 36 sts total (see page 15). Divide sts onto 4 dpn and work as shown on thumb chart. Cut yarn and draw end through rem sts; tighten.

Left Mitten
Work mirror-image from chart.

Finishing
Weave in all ends neatly on WS. Gently steam press under a damp pressing cloth to block.

King of the Forest

Animal figures have always been very popular in Norwegian knitwear, and deer and birds are among the most used. Moose, deer, and reindeer on knitted garments are almost national symbols.

Inspiration and pattern elements were often drawn from samplers. Everything that can be sewn with cross stitch can also be adapted for weaving or knitting patterns. Samplers have been worked in Norway since the beginning of the 1700s. They were a useful aid in the traditional handwork education of girls. From a pedagogic viewpoint, it was two birds with one stone: girls learned the alphabet and basic embroidery skills at the same time. Samplers also functioned as a type of pattern collection. In addition to letters and numbers, they usually featured small motifs—Adam and Eve in the Garden of Eden, flowers, trees, and various animals, eight-petaled roses, and all kinds of decorative borders.

The motifs on samplers could have been taken from the foreign pattern booklets or notebooks that became increasingly popular by the end of the nineteenth century. Many of the knitting patterns we label "Norwegian" today came precisely from these sources. The panel between the cuff and mitten on the women's mitten with the "weathervane rose" on page 136 is an example. We can also find these popular pattern panels in a German pattern booklet from the late nineteenth century.

Moose, deer, and reindeer on knitted garments are often rendered in some detail. Annichen Sibbern Bøhn has, for example, a large stag with impressive antlers in her book *Norwegian Knitting Patterns*, which came out in 1928. I let myself be inspired by many of the enjoyable animal motifs, but have chosen to use a tighter and more stylized form for my moose.

The Norwegian Folk Museum has a pair of mittens with the date (1895) knitted in. A large deer with impressive antlers decorates almost the entire surface.

Thumb

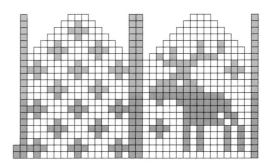

☐ White—knit
▨ Gray—knit

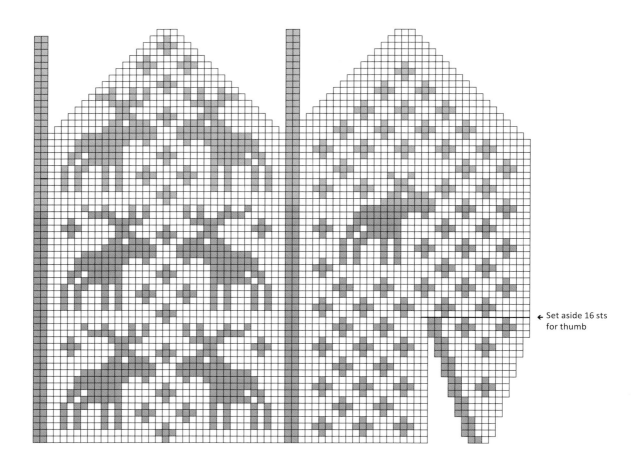

← Set aside 16 sts
for thumb

In 1953, the Norwegian Weekly Magazine published a pattern book-let that quickly became very popular. This is my mother, photographed in a newly-knitted sweater with rein-deer. She wanted to have it ready for the Easter holiday at Geilo the same year. She was 15 years old at the time.

INSTRUCTIONS

Sizes: Women's (Men's)

MATERIALS
Yarn:
CYCA #1 (fingering), 2-ply Gammelserie from Rauma (100% wool, 175 yd/160 m / 50 g), Gray 405: 50 (100) g
CYCA #1 (light fingering), Lamullgarn from Rauma (100% wool (273 yd/250 m / 50 g), White L11: 50 (100) g

Needles: U.S. size 1.5 (2.5) / 2.5 (3) mm, set of 5 dpn

Gauge: 32 (29) sts = 4 in / 10 cm.
Adjust needle size to obtain correct gauge if necessary.

Right Mitten
With White, CO 60 sts and divide sts evenly over 4 dpn. Join to work in the round. Work around in k1, p1 ribbing for 3¼ in / 8.5 cm). After ribbing is complete, change to St st,

increase 1 st to 61 sts, and continue in St st following charted pattern. Increase as shown for the thumb gusset. At dark line, set aside 16 sts for the thumb (see page 15 for details). Continue, shaping top of mitten as shown on chart (see page 13 for details). Cut yarn and draw end through rem sts; tighten.

Thumb
Pick up and knit 18 + 18 sts around thumb-hole = 36 sts total (see page 15). Divide sts onto 4 dpn and work as shown on thumb chart. Cut yarn and draw end through rem sts; tighten.

Left Mitten
Work mirror-image from chart.

Finishing
Weave in all ends neatly on WS. Gently steam press under a damp pressing cloth to block.

Striped Mittens from Østerdalen

In conjunction with a collection for a big knitting exhibition in 1984, Drude Andersen (born in 1924) related that this type of striped mitten was previously very common in Østerdalen. They were always knitted in black and white; there are several similarities with the better-known Hadeland mitten, but the stripes are made differently and the cuff is also different.

It was common to knit initials and the date in the white area. I've chosen to knit in my first name with small letters on both the outside and the inside—but you can do what you like!

According to the archive records, this pair of mittens was originally knitted in 1968 by Karen Asphaug (born about 1900) from Stor-Elvdal. Drude Andersen from Hamar learned the technique from her. New mittens with the same pattern were knitted on the old cuffs in 1981.

Thumb

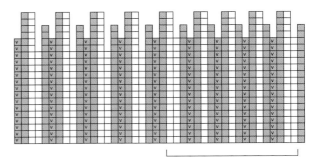

Front

□ White—knit
▨ Red—knit
▾ Red—purl
⊡ Inc 1 st with Red
⊡ Inc 1 st with White

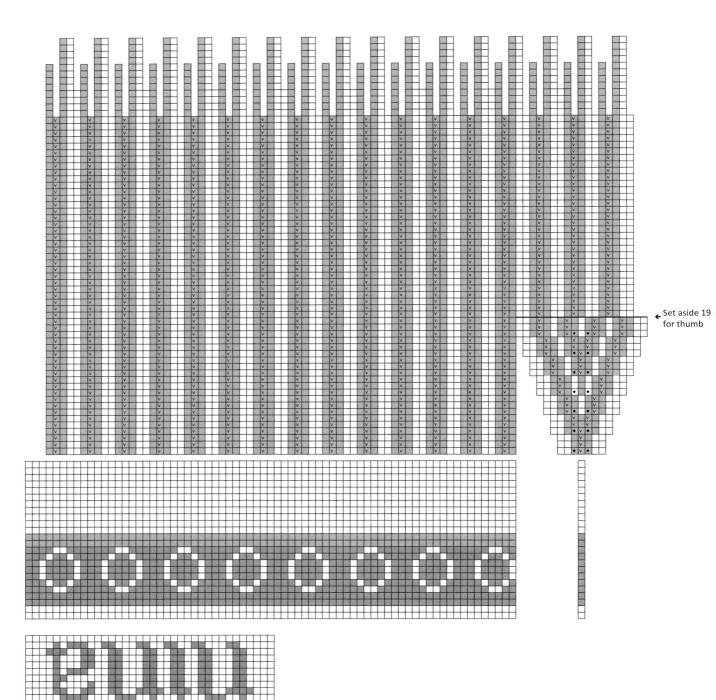

← Set aside 19 for thumb

INSTRUCTIONS

Sizes: Women's (Men's)

MATERIALS
Yarn:
CYCA #1 (fingering), Dale Baby Ull (100% wool, 180 yd/165 m / 50 g)

Yarn Amounts
Red 4018: 50 (100) g
White 0017: 50 (100) g

Needles: U.S. size 1.5 (2.5) / 2.5 (3) mm, set of 5 dpn

Gauge: 33 (30) sts = 4 in / 10 cm.
Adjust needle size to obtain correct gauge if necessary.

Right Mitten
With White, CO 72 sts and divide sts evenly over 4 dpn. Join to work in the round. Work around in St st for ⅜ in / 1 cm. Now work an eyelet rnd for foldline: (K2tog, yo) around. Continue in St st as shown on the chart. Fill the White band with your name, initials, or the year.

Before you begin the stripes, inc 3 sts evenly spaced around = 75 sts rem. The repeat is 5 sts—the center st is always Red and purled. Continue, increasing for the thumb gusset as indicated on the chart. At the dark line, place the 19 thumb sts on a holder. CO 17 sts over the gap. Continue, shaping top of mitten as shown on chart (see page 13 for details). Cut yarn and draw end through rem sts; tighten.

Thumb
Pick up and knit 21 + 21 sts around thumb-hole = 42 sts total. Divide sts onto 4 dpn and work as shown on thumb chart. Cut yarn and draw end through rem sts; tighten.

Left Mitten
Work mirror-image from chart.

Finishing
Fold cuff at eyelet rnd and loosely sew down on WS. Weave in all ends neatly on WS. Gently steam press under a damp pressing cloth to block.

Rose Mittens from Skjåk

Among the items registered in connection with the exhibition "Knitting Then and Now" in 1984 are a pair of men's mittens from Skjåk, which are locally called rose mittens. They were knitted with black and white handspun yarn. The mittens had been well-used and are a little scorched. According to the registration card, there is a large darned area on the palm. The mittens were knitted by Marit Øyastugu Garmo (1855-1944) around 1900, and the pattern is considered hers.

In the 1900 census for the township of Lom, we find her listed as Marit Olsdatter from Skjåk. She was a farmer's wife, married to Ivar Stuen at the farm with the same name. They grew grain and potatoes, and had farm animals and poultry, but no beehives, kitchen, or fruit garden. Living at their home was one daughter, who was a dairymaid; 7 sons; and 1 pensioner—Marit's 88-year-old father.

In the same census, we find there were many women living on farms in the area, widows, and unmarried women who had "spinsters" and "knitters" listed as their occupations.

Erling Bjørk (born in 1913) owned these mittens. The decoratively patterned cuffs were typical for men's mittens in the district. Women's mittens had a simpler, striped cuff. Several women in Skjåk knitted the same rose-patterned mittens.

Thumb

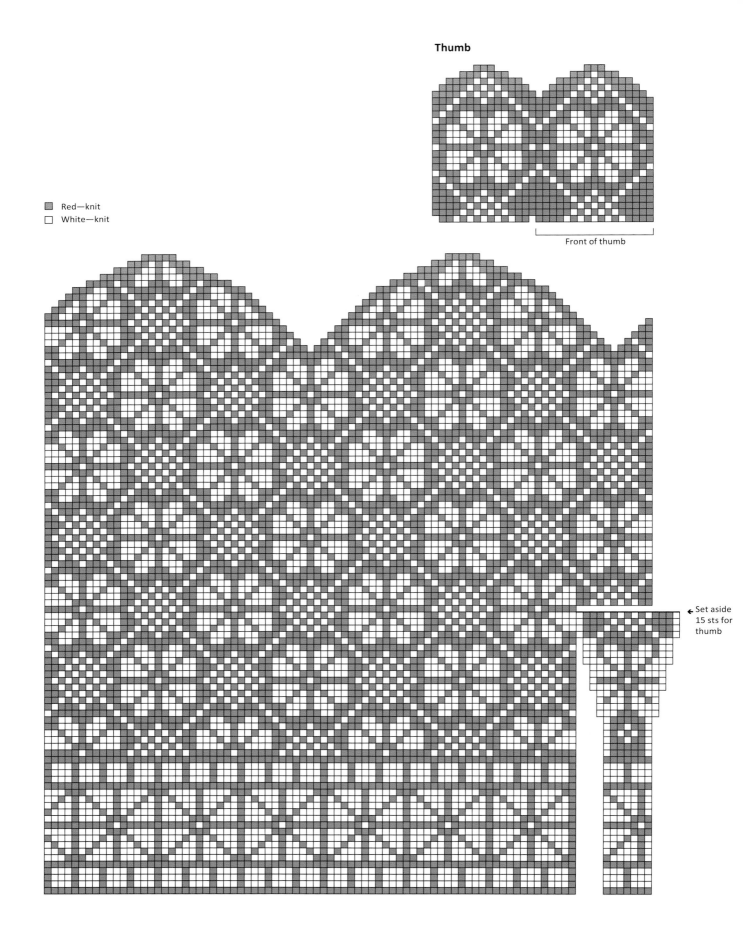

Front of thumb

■ Red—knit
□ White—knit

← Set aside 15 sts for thumb

INSTRUCTIONS

Sizes: Women's (Men's)

MATERIALS
Yarn:
CYCA #1 (fingering), Dale Baby Ull (100% Merino wool, 180 yd/165 m / 50 g)

Yarn Amounts
Red 4018: 50 (100) g
White 0017: 50 (100) g

Needles: U.S. size 0 (1.5) / 2 (2.5) mm, set of 5 dpn

Gauge: 38 (34) sts = 4 in / 10 cm.
Adjust needle size to obtain correct gauge if necessary.

Right Mitten
With Red over the thumb and White over index finger, use the long-tail method to CO 84 sts and divide sts evenly over 4 dpn. Join to work in the round. Work 1 rnd two-end purl braid (see page 14). Continue in St st following the chart.

Increase for the thumb gusset as shown and, at the dark line, place the 15 thumb sts on a holder. CO 11 sts over the gap on the next rnd.

Continue, shaping top of mitten as shown on chart (see page 13 for details). Cut yarn and draw end through rem sts; tighten.

Thumb
Pick up and knit 17 + 13 sts around thumbhole = 30 sts total. Divide sts onto 4 dpn and work in St st as shown on thumb chart. On the second rnd, inc 2 sts on the back of the thumb as indicated on chart. Cut yarn and draw end through rem sts; tighten.

Left Mitten
Work mirror-image from chart.

Finishing
Weave in all ends neatly on WS. Gently steam press under a damp pressing cloth to block.

Heart Brooch Mittens

In previous times, it was common to knit both while standing and while walking. Every free moment had to be used. In order to hold the yarn strands correctly, a ball hook hanging from a belt, apron, or jacket was used. It was a very simple but practical tool.

Ball hooks were often made of brass but some were iron or a combination of iron and brass. The finest were silver. Although they were small, they were often decorated—with small figures, a girl's name, or the year.

The hook was hung on a belt, with the yarn ball held in with a simple latch at the bottom. This arrangement was advantageous because the yarn could be drawn out from the center of the ball, especially if the ball had been wound on a winding stick (*nøstepinne*).

The pattern for these mittens was inspired by an elegant heart brooch. Heart brooches have been used to decorate folk costumes all around Norway, although the shape varies quite a bit from province to province. Brooches were often decorated with a crown at the top. It's also common to find a crown over a heart on old samplers—where it was a symbol of devotion.

Swedish photographer Axel Lindahl (1841-1906) traveled around Norway between 1883 and 1889. Here he's captured everyday life in Hardanger.

Thumb

☐ White—knit
▨ Red—knit
ⓥ White—purl
▨ Red—purl

← Set aside 16 sts for thumb

50

INSTRUCTIONS

Sizes: Women's (Men's)

MATERIALS
Yarn:
CYCA #1 (fingering), Dale Baby Ull (100% Merino wool, 180 yd/165 m / 50 g)

Yarn Amounts
Red 4018: 50 (100) g
White 0010: 50 (100) g

Needles: U.S. size 0 (1.5) / 2 (2.5) mm, set of 5 dpn

Gauge: 35 (32) sts = 4 in / 10 cm.
Adjust needle size to obtain correct gauge if necessary.

Right Mitten
With Red, CO 64 sts and divide sts evenly over 4 dpn. Join to work in the round. Work 2 rnds of staggered ribbing as shown on the chart. Change to White and continue staggered rib as charted. After completing

ribbing, continue in St st and pattern following the chart.

Increase for the thumb gusset as shown and, at the dark line, place the 16 thumb sts on a holder. CO 15 sts over the gap on the next rnd.

Continue, shaping top of mitten as shown on chart (see page 13 for details). Cut yarn and draw end through rem sts; tighten.

Thumb
Pick up and knit 17 + 17 sts around thumbhole = 34 sts total. Divide sts onto 4 dpn and work as shown on thumb chart. Cut yarn and draw end through rem sts; tighten.

Left Mitten
Work mirror-image from chart.

Finishing
Weave in all ends neatly on WS. Gently steam press under a damp pressing cloth to block.

Driving Mittens from Flesberg

A pair of sturdy driving mittens from Flesberg was among the items registered in connection with the large traveling exhibition "Knitting Then and Now"—a collaboration between the Norwegian Handcraft Association and the Norwegian Folk Museum. The mittens belonged to Kittil Værås of Nordre Aslefet. They were knitted with handspun yarn in black and white and then dyed green. The bottom edges were covered with a shag fringe. The mittens are lined with a second pair of stockinette-knitted mittens without any patterning, felted after knitting. The registration card notes that the mittens were in good condition but the right mitten was darned on the tip. The pair weighed a hefty 12.3 ounces / 350 grams.

The Norwegian Handcrafts Organization declared that all the valuable resources and materials that had been collected between September 1983 and September 1984 should be available for the enjoyment of the larger public. Everything was photographed and catalogued for the book Knitting in Norway. The material was transferred to the Norwegian Folk Museum "to be available for study purposes of anyone interested."

Thumb

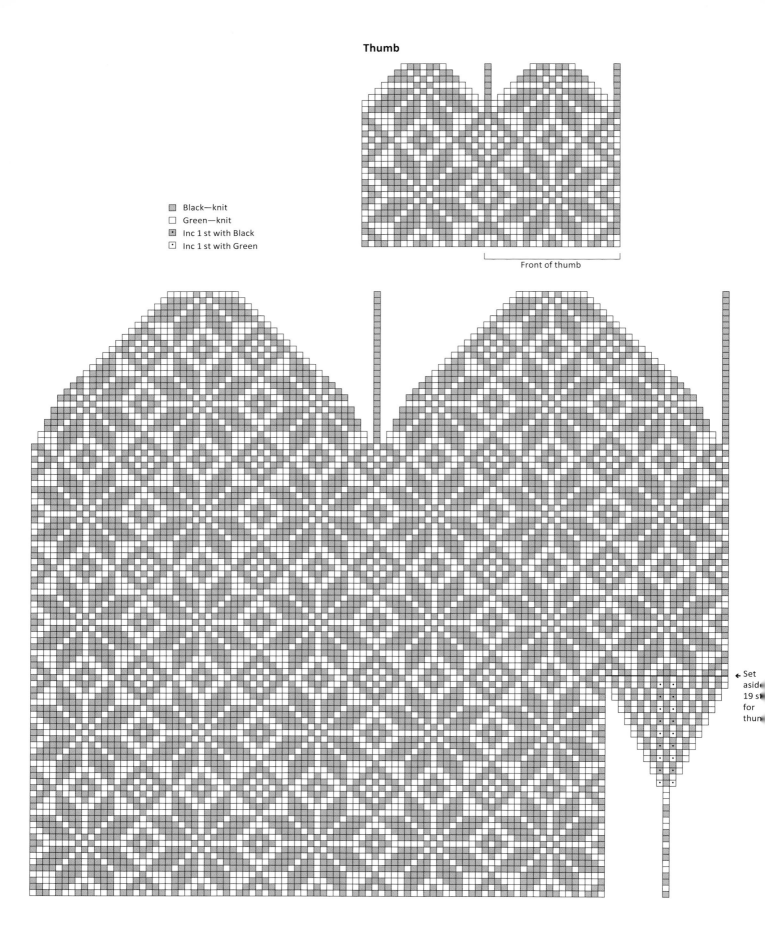

- Black—knit
- Green—knit
- Inc 1 st with Black
- Inc 1 st with Green

Front of thumb

← Set aside 19 sts for thumb

54

INSTRUCTIONS

Sizes: Women's (Men's)

MATERIALS
Yarn:
CYCA #2 (sport), Fine 2-ply Old Spelsau wool yarn from Selbu Spinneri (can be substituted with Ask / Hifa 2 from Hillesvåg) (100% wool, 345 yd/315 m / 100 g), Black: 100 (100) g
CYCA #1 (fingering), Røros embroidery yarn from Rauma (100% Spelsau wool, 547 yd/500 m / 100 g), Green 383 or specially dyed green from the Bergen Handcraft Association: 100 (100) g
CYCA #1 (fingering), two-ply Gammelserie from Rauma (100% wool, 175 yd/160 m / 50 g), Blue 446: 50 (50) g

Needles: U.S. size 000 (0) / 1.5 (2) mm, set of 5 dpn

Gauge: 46 (41) sts = 4 in / 10 cm.
Adjust needle size to obtain correct gauge if necessary.

Right Mitten
With Black, CO 90 sts and divide sts over 4 dpn. Join to work in the round. *Work 2 rnds of k2, p2 ribbing and then work 2 rnds p2, k2 ribbing*. Rep * to * 3 times. Continue in St st with Black and Green following the chart.

Increase for the thumb gusset on each side of a center st to form stripes. At the dark line, set aside 19 sts for the thumb (see page 15 for details).

Continue, shaping top of mitten as shown on chart (see page 13 for details). Cut yarn and draw end through rem sts; tighten.

Thumb
Pick up and knit 20 + 20 sts around thumb-hole = 40 sts total (see page 15). Divide sts onto 4 dpn and work as shown on thumb chart. Cut yarn and draw end through rem sts; tighten.

Left Mitten
Work mirror-image from chart.

Finishing
Weave in all ends neatly on WS. Gently steam press under a damp pressing cloth to block.

Shag fringe: Thread 1 green and 1 blue strand doubled in a tapestry needle. Sew vertical rows of horizontal stitches tightly spaced over a knitting needle U.S. size 8 or 9 (4.5 or 5 mm) held over RS of knitting. The stitches should lie inside the work on the wrong side and the loops on the right side when you draw the needle out. Continue around until the entire cuff is covered. Cut the loops open and trim them evenly with sharp scissors.

Mittens from Hallingdal

Hallingdal Museum has a pair of mittens from Knut Knutson Heje of Flå. It is hard to say whether he was the oldest son and heir of Heie estate, the agronomist and editor who lived from 1852 until 1942, or the brother eight years younger with the same name. The two were often confused. The latter was the mayor of Flå and later the parliamentary representative for Venstre.

The mittens were knitted with a strong 3-ply handspun wool yarn in natural black and white and embellished with a fringe around the wrist. On the outer side of the cuffs, the initials KKSH are knitted in. The mittens are well-worn and have some holes—they were likely attacked by moths. Some spots have been darned.

The majority of the knitted garments preserved from Hallingdal are worked in one color and decorated with rich embroidery. This pair of mittens is distinguished by its simple but distinct two-color pattern.

Thumb

White—knit
Gray—knit

Front of thumb

← Set aside
25 sts for
thumb

58

If you want to be proficient at knitting, you have to start young. It wasn't always fun. "Mother's instruction" is the name of this photo, taken by Knud Knudsen in 1875 or 1876.

INSTRUCTIONS

Sizes: Women's (Men's)

MATERIALS
Yarn:
CYCA #1 (fingering), two-ply Spelsau from Hoelfeldt-Lund (100% wool, 244 yd/223 m / 50 g) OR Norsk Pelsull from Hillesvåg (CYCA #3 [DK/light worsted], 100% wool, 284 yd/260 m / 100 g)

Yarn Amounts
Dark Gray (natural color): 100 (100) g
Light Gray (natural color): 100 (100) g

Needles: U.S. size 0 (1.5) / 2 (2.5) mm, set of 5 dpn

Gauge: 34 (31) sts = 4 in / 10 cm.
Adjust needle size to obtain correct gauge if necessary.

Right Mitten
With Dark Gray over the thumb and Light Gray over the index finger, use the long-tail cast-on method to CO 72 sts. Divide sts over 4 dpn and join to work in the round. Work 1 rnd two-end purl braid (see page 14). Continue in St st following the chart.

Increase for the thumb gusset as indicated on chart. At the dark line, place the 25 thumb sts on a holder. CO 10 sts over the gap on the next rnd.

Continue, shaping top of mitten as shown on chart (see page 13 for details). Cut yarn and draw end through rem sts; tighten.

Thumb
Pick up and knit 27 + 13 sts around thumbhole = 40 sts total. Make sure that the pattern is correctly aligned over the sts held for the thumb. Divide sts onto 4 dpn and work as shown on thumb chart. Cut yarn and draw end through rem sts; tighten.

Left Mitten
Work mirror-image from chart.

Finishing
Weave in all ends neatly on WS. Gently steam press under a damp pressing cloth to block.

Porcelain Flowers

In olden days, if you wanted to dye some wool blue, you had to use a plant called woad, which yielded an indigo dye matter, or authentic indigo from *indigofera anil*, introduced from the tropics. Synthetic indigo came on the market in about 1900.

Indigo has to be diluted in an ammonia bath. Urine was used for this—hence the name "pot blue." Male urine was preferred because urine from women might contain egg white, which could affect the color.

The blue color used to decorate porcelain was derived from cobalt. From the end of the 18th century up until about 1900, when Norway was a poor country on the edge of Europe, the royal blue color was extracted from cobalt ore on Modum in Buskerud. The highest quality of this dye powder was sent from the Blue Dye Works to customers all over Europe, and even faraway countries such as China and Japan. In the 1830s, it was Norway's largest industrial company.

These mittens were inspired by the blue flowers often seen on Danish, German, and Norwegian porcelain.

Here we can see how the wool was dyed at the Arne factory in 1932. Sometimes raw wool was dyed and sometimes yarn. A third option was to dye the finished knitted garment.

Thumb

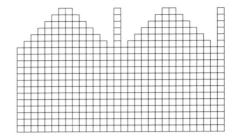

□ White—knit
▨ Blue—knit
ⱴ White—purl
ⱴ Blue—purl

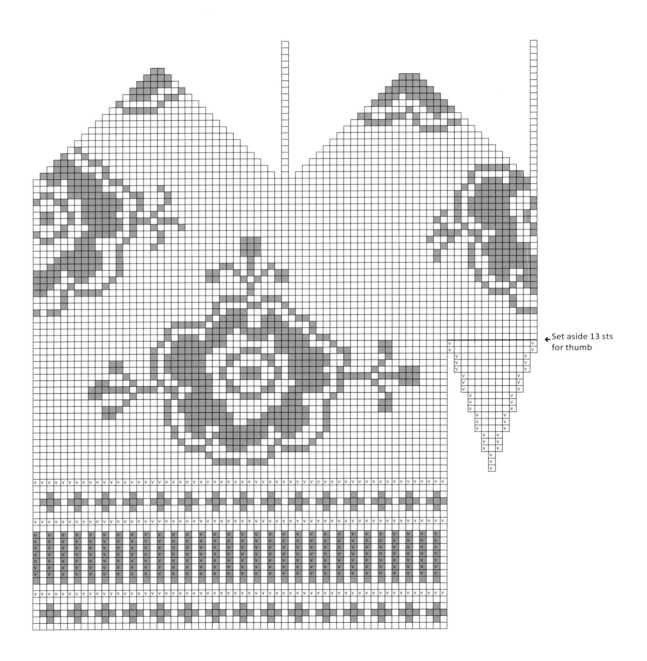

← Set aside 13 sts
for thumb

INSTRUCTIONS

Sizes: Women's (Men's)

MATERIALS
Yarn:
CYCA #2 (sport), PT5 from Rauma (80% wool, 20% polyamide, 140 yd/128 m / 50 g)

Yarn Amounts
Blue 567: 50 (100) g
White 502: 50 (100) g

Needles: U.S. size 2.5 (4) / 3 (3.5) mm, set of 5 dpn

Gauge: 27 (24) sts = 4 in / 10 cm.
Adjust needle size to obtain correct gauge if necessary.

NOTE: This design has long yarn floats. For best results, you should twist the white and blue strands around each other on the wrong side on about every sixth stitch. On the next round, stagger the twist to the left or to the right to avoid stacking the twists above each other. Stacked yarn twists will show through on the right side.

Right Mitten
With White, CO 60 sts. Divide sts over 4 dpn and join to work in the round. Knit 1 rnd and then purl 1 rnd. Continue with knit and purl sts as indicated on the chart.

Increase for the thumb gusset as indicated on chart. At the dark line, set aside 13 sts for the thumb (see page 15 for details).

Continue, shaping top of mitten as shown on chart (see page 13 for details). Cut yarn and draw end through rem sts; tighten.

Thumb
With White, pick up and knit 30 sts around thumbhole. Divide sts onto 4 dpn and work as shown on thumb chart. Cut yarn and draw end through rem sts; tighten.

Left Mitten
Work mirror-image from chart.

Finishing
Weave in all ends neatly on WS. Gently steam press under a damp pressing cloth to block.

Vestfold Mittens

In the autumn of 1987, I was a newly-employed journalist at the Norwegian handcraft magazine *Husflid*. In preparation for a themed issue on mittens, I got in touch with my design instructor at the State Teacher's College, Ingebjørg Gravjord, to find out if she could contribute a pattern. The year before, Ingebjørg had published her book *Votten i norsk tradisjon* [Mittens in the Norwegian Tradition]. She suggested that we publish a simplified version of the Vestfold mitten pattern—a pretty mitten with a cable design that had come to light in connection with the exhibition "Knitting Then and Now" in Tønsberg in 1983. Ingebjørg had come upon the pattern a few months earlier when she was searching in the archives at the Norwegian Handcraft Association in Oslo. In the scant information, it stated that the pattern had been printed at Amtstidenes Printing. Jarlsberg and Laurvig's Amtstidende came out in Larvik between 1834 and 1940.

The pattern republished by *Husflid* was very simplified. The attractive cuff was substituted with a regular ribbed cuff. In addition, it had so many errors and omissions that it was impossible to knit following the instructions. Therefore, the mitten has been reconstructed following the picture in Ingebjørg's book.

INSTRUCTIONS

Sizes: Women's

MATERIALS
Yarn:
CYCA #1 (fingering), Babyull Lanett Superwash from Sandnes Garn (100% Merino wool, 191 yd/175 m / 50 g), Pink 4312: 150 g

Needles: U.S. size 0 / 2 mm, set of 5 dpn; cable needle

Gauge: 32 sts = 4 in / 10 cm.
Adjust needle size to obtain correct gauge if necessary.

Right Mitten
CO 76 sts. Divide sts over 4 dpn and join to work in the round. Work following the chart. The pattern repeat is worked over 34 rnds.

As indicated on the chart, 8 sts are increased for the thumb gusset, two sts in from the patterning. At the dark line, set aside 15 sts for the thumb (see page 15 for details).

Continue, shaping top of mitten as shown on chart (see page 13 for details). Cut yarn and draw end through rem sts; tighten.

Thumb
Pick up and knit 17 + 17 sts around thumbhole = 34 sts total (see page 15). Divide sts onto 4 dpn and work in St st as shown on thumb chart. Cut yarn and draw end through rem sts; tighten.

Cuff
CO 42 sts and work back and forth following the chart. The first row is purled. The cables are worked on the RS and all sts are purled on WS.

Left Mitten
Work mirror-image from chart. The cuff is worked the same way for both mittens.

Finishing
Weave in all ends neatly on WS. Fold the cuff in half and sew it together along the diagonal line using mattress stitch. Sew a cuff to each mitten.

Blocking
With the cables facing up, pin out the mittens to finished size. Spray with water until lightly damp and leave to dry for about a day.

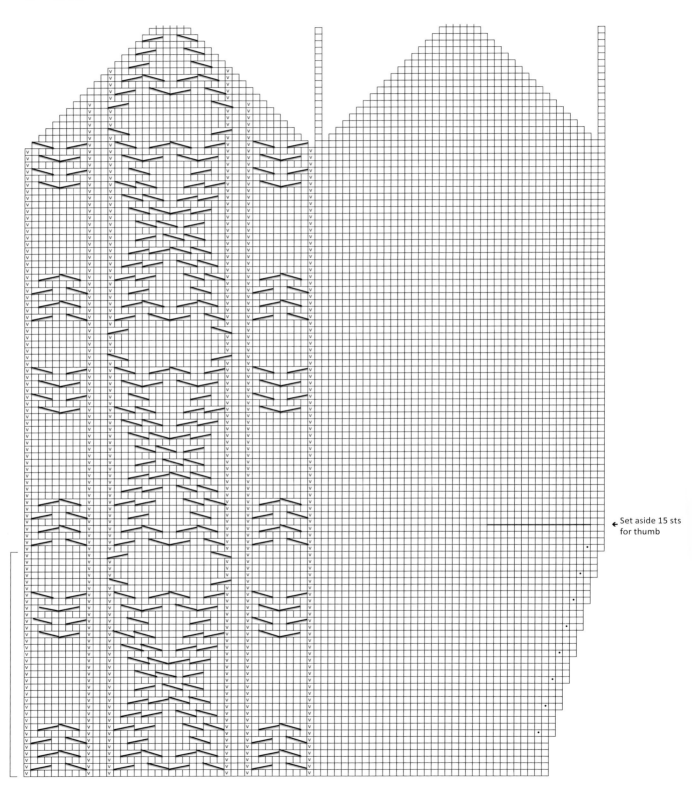

Knit

 Purl

Sl 1 st to cable needle and hold in back of work, k2 and then k1 from cable needle

Sl 2 sts to cable needle and hold in front of work, k1 and then k2 from cable needle

Inc 1 st

Set aside 15 sts for thumb

Cuff

Thumb

Repeat
2 times

Mittens from West Telemark

Early on, Rikhard Berge (1888-1969) from Rauland in Telemark was interested in folk-lore and objects from the countryside. A child's or woman's mitten in fine violet and pink wool yarn was among the first items he collected. However, he must not have had much knowledge about textile techniques. In his own records, it says "1 pair even blue child's mittens with red rose stitching (Sauma by Svanaug Hallvardsdatter Lid)". It could mean that embroidered mittens were more common than pattern-knitted ones in Telemark.

Svanaug Hallvardsdatter Lid came from Øyfjell in Vinje. She was born sometime between 1823 and 1828 as the third child in a large family. Together with her husband, Olav Ånundson Trovatn, she immigrated to America in 1862. The mitten was most likely knitted before then. It's among the oldest pattern knitted textiles we know about in the country.

The mitten has a characteristic shag fringe around the wrist and now belongs to the West-Telemark Museum. It is only 8 inches / 20 centimeters long and knitted at a gauge of 44 stitches in 4 inches / 10 centimeters. The palm is darned with orange and brown wool yarn. I decided to make the new mitten a little larger.

In the book *Knitting from Great Grandmother's Time* (1910), there's a pattern for the same mitten—but it's called a "Mitten from Hallingdal." Perhaps the author met Rikhard Berge?

The West-Telemark Museum has a mitten—either a small woman's mitten, or else a large child's size. It features a pretty eight-petaled rose and shag fringe around the wrist. According to folklore collector Rikard Berge, it was made by Svanaug Halvardsdatter Lid, who immigrated to America in 1862.

Thumb

Fringe

☐ Red—knit
▨ Black—knit

← Set aside
19 sts for
thumb

Shag fringe

INSTRUCTIONS

Sizes: Women's (Men's)

MATERIALS
Yarn:
CYCA #1 (fingering), 2-ply Gammelserie from Rauma (100% wool, 175 yd/160 m / 50 g)

Yarn Amounts
Black 436: 50 (100) g
Red 424: 50 (100) g

Needles: U.S. size 0 (1.5) / 2 (2.5) mm, set of 5 dpn

Gauge: 37 (33) sts = 4 in / 10 cm.
Adjust needle size to obtain correct gauge if necessary.

Right Mitten
With 2 strands of Red, use the long-tail cast-on method to CO 74 sts. Divide sts over 4 dpn and join to work in the round. Work 1 rnd two-end purl braid (see page 14). Change to Black and knit 2 rnds. Change to Red and knit 1 rnd, purl 1 rnd, knit 2 rnds. Continue, following the chart.

When you are halfway in the rose panel,

increase a total of 14 sts spaced as shown on chart = 88 sts total.

At dark line on chart, set aside 19 thumb sts for the thumb (see page 15 for details).

Continue, shaping top of mitten as shown on chart (see page 13 for details). Cut yarn and draw end through rem sts; tighten.

Thumb
Pick up and knit 21 sts on each side of waste yarn (see page 15). Divide sts onto 4 dpn and work as shown on thumb chart. Cut yarn and draw end through rem sts; tighten.

Left Mitten
Work mirror-image from chart.

Finishing
If you want to copy the fringe as on the original mitten, place it on the rows marked on the chart. You can use simple Turkish knots—a technique borrowed from weaving.
Weave in all ends neatly on WS.
Gently steam press under a damp pressing cloth to block.

Children's Mittens from Setesdal

Norwegian national and folk costumes in Fagernes have registered a little red child's mitten from Valle in Setesdal. The mitten has the same type of cable pattern also found on stockings from that district. The locals call the stockings *krotasokker*—*krot* means "pattern".

Garments were often knitted with white sheep's wool and then dyed after the knitting was complete. That was, as a rule, easier then dyeing yarn skeins. The red dye used to come from madder plants, which had to be cultivated, or *galium boreale tormentil*, which grew wild. The roots of the plants were the parts used. For a more blueish-red color, the scales of cochineal lice could be used. These lice live on cactus plants in warm climates and must be imported. Today, the dye from cochineal is used in both food and cosmetics.

Many mittens preserved from Setesdal have cable and wave patterns. This little child's mitten is somewhat unusual, with patterns closely related to those on the stockings knitted in the valley.

□ Knit

□ Twisted knit (knit through back loop)

v Purl

▧ K2tog tbl without slipping them off left needle, knit the 1st st again and then slip both sts off needle

▨ K2tog tbl without slipping them off left needle, knit the 1st st again and then slip both sts off needle

v▭ Sl 1 st to cable needle and hold in front of work, p2, k1 tbl from cable needle

v▭ Sl 1 st to cable needle and hold in back of work, k2 tbl, p1 from cable needle

▭ Sl 1 st to cable needle and hold in back of work, k2 tbl, k1 tbl from cable needle

Thumb

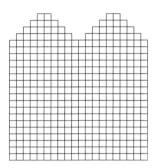

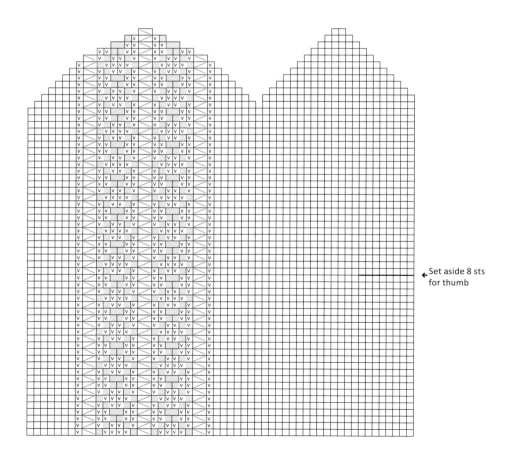

← Set aside 8 sts for thumb

INSTRUCTIONS

Sizes: 6 (8) years

MATERIALS
Yarn:
CYCA #1 (fingering), Finullgarn from Rauma (100% wool, 191 yd/175 m / 50 g), Coral 469: 50 (50) g

Needles: U.S. size 0 (1.5) / 2 (2.5) mm, set of 5 dpn; cable needle

Gauge: 28 (27) sts = 4 in / 10 cm.
Adjust needle size to obtain correct gauge if necessary.

Right Mitten
CO 56 sts. Divide sts over 4 dpn and join to work in the round. Work 12 rnds in twisted rib: (k1 tbl, p1) around. Continue in St st and cable pattern, following the chart.
At the dark line, set aside 8 sts for the thumb (see page 15 for details).

Continue, shaping top of mitten as shown on chart (see page 13 for details). Cut yarn and draw end through rem sts; tighten.

Thumb
Pick up and knit 10 + 10 sts around thumbhole = 20 sts total (see page 15). Divide sts onto 4 dpn and work as shown on thumb chart. Cut yarn and draw end through rem sts; tighten.

Left Mitten
Work mirror-image from chart.

Finishing
Weave in all ends neatly on WS. Very gently steam press under a damp pressing cloth to block, making sure the cables are not flattened.

75

Mittens from Kristiansand

A while ago, it was common to leave old and worn textiles at the shoddy mill for recycling and reuse. The materials were shredded and then carded and spun into new yarn, or used as filling for quilts and mattresses. This is the reason why so few textile materials have been preserved. Wool was far too valuable not to use again.

In 1983, Annemor Sundbø bought a shoddy mill by the name of Torridal Tweed and Wool Comforter Factory in Kristiansand—and its sixteen tons of old knitted garments. She meticulously sorted through the piles and, in a series of books and articles, she documented much of Norwegian knitting history. The Norwegian Handcraft Association's large knitting exhibition in 1984 included a mitten she'd donated to the West-Agder Museum. It was knitted with handspun yarn and had a lovely floral pattern. The panel on the cuff was taken from Annichen Sibbern Bøhn's pattern book, first published in 1928. I've reconstructed the pattern, but decided to use a single color for the ribbed panel between the cuff and hand, which was originally striped.

Knitting women have always been quick to adopt new pattern panels. This cuff pattern was very popular after Annichen Sibbern Bøhn published her pattern collection in 1928. It's difficult to determine where the lovely flower vine pattern came from, but it's a stylized version of the pretty but oh-so-poisonous foxglove.

Thumb

Chart 2

← Set aside 17 sts
for thumb

Chart 1

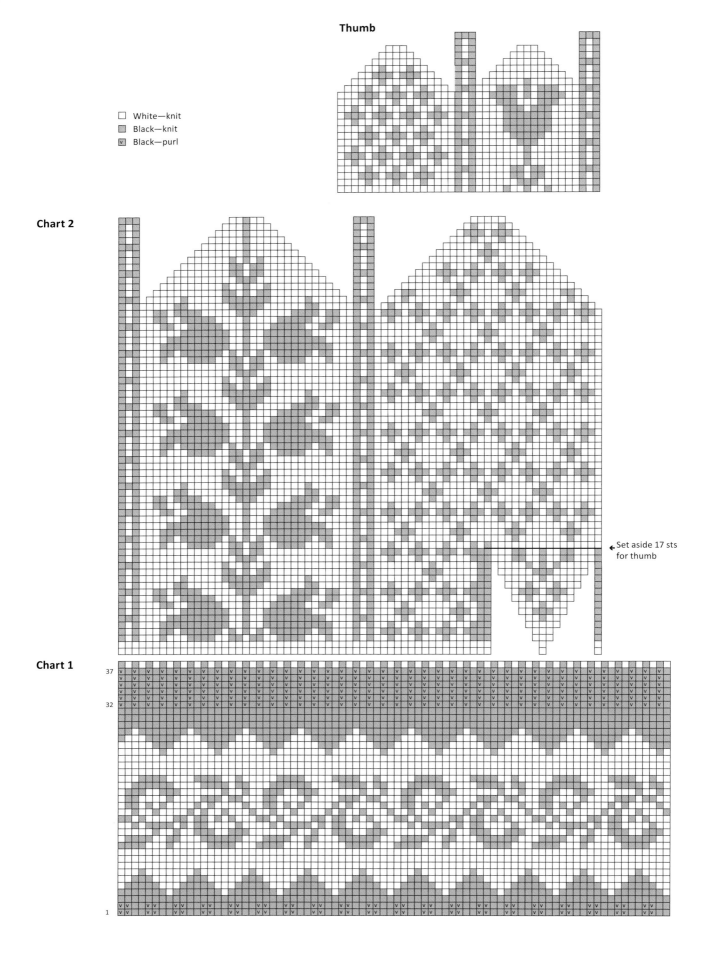

78

INSTRUCTIONS

Sizes: Women's (Men's)

MATERIALS
Yarn:
CYCA #1 (fingering), 2-ply Gammelserie from Rauma (100% wool, 175 yd/160 m / 50 g)

Yarn Amounts
Black 436: 50 (100) g
White 400: 50 (100) g

Needles: U.S. size 0 (1.5) / 2 (2.5) mm, set of 5 dpn

Gauge: 32 (29) sts = 4 in / 10 cm.
Adjust needle size to obtain correct gauge if necessary.

Right Mitten
With Black, CO 80 sts. Divide sts over 4 dpn and join to work in the round. Work 2 rnds in k2, p2 ribbing. Continue in St st, following Chart 1 (cuff). On Rnds 32 through 37, work in k1, p1 ribbing as shown.

Continue in St st. On Rnd 39, decrease evenly spaced around to 56 sts. Begin Chart 2, increasing for the thumb gusset as shown. At the dark line, set aside 17 thumb sts for the thumb (see page 15 for details).

Continue, shaping top of mitten as shown on chart (see page 13 for details). Cut yarn and draw end through rem sts; tighten.

Thumb
Pick up and knit 19 + 19 sts around thumb-hole = 38 sts total (see page 15). Divide sts onto 4 dpn and work as shown on thumb chart. Cut yarn and draw end through rem sts; tighten.

Left Mitten
Work mirror-image from chart.

Finishing
Weave in all ends neatly on WS. Gently steam press under a damp pressing cloth to block.

Witchcraft Mittens

Lisbet Pedersdatter is the first Norwegian knitter we know about. Lisbet was accused of witchcraft, and the case against her was held in Jenns Thommesen's house in Stavanger on August 22, 1634. From the legal records, we know she made her living knitting stockings.

Her name is among a total of 860 people accused of witchcraft in Norway in the 1500s and 1600s; 307 of them were executed. Most of those executed were women who were burned alive. The majority of those put on trial for witchcraft were people who owned little or nothing and were outside acceptable social classes. Quite often they were also indicted for other offenses.

Lisbet—who was from Kristiania—was in service at the home of Karen Eriksdatter of Leikanger, in Sogn. Lisbet received clothing and food in exchange for "doing chores and knitting stockings." She was considered a "tramp."

Karen was, in the meantime, accused and imprisoned for theft of some children's clothing. She was sentenced to lose some skin, probably by whipping, or to leave Stavanger within three days.

Lisbet was accused because an eagle's foot had been found in a bag she carried. Lisbet claimed it was intended to help an itching on her thighs, and she didn't know anything about witchcraft—and she must have been believed, because she wasn't convicted.

Knitting had established a solid foothold on Iceland and the Faroe Islands by the 1500s, and was also known about in Denmark—and probably Sweden, at about the same time. We don't know where and how Lisbet learned to knit stockings, but clearly knitting was common enough to be assigned as work for those at the lowest social level.

I made these mittens to honor all those who were wrongfully accused of witchcraft—hence the name "Witchcraft Mittens." I got the idea for the pattern as I knitted the Folk Museum's Selbu mittens shown on page 144. I thought the cuffs on those mittens were so fine that I couldn't resist working with the pattern elements a bit more.

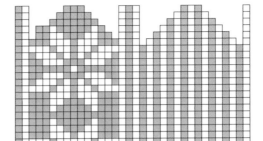

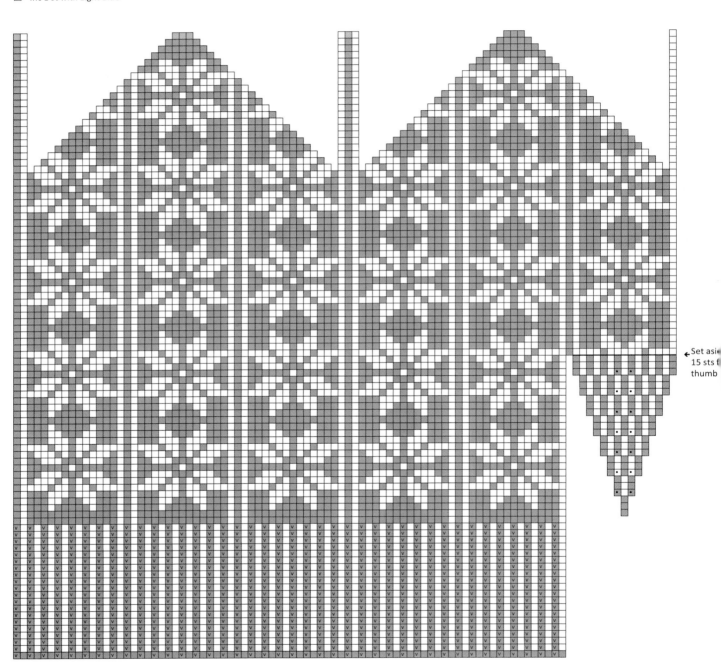

- Gray—knit
- Gray—purl
- Light Blue—knit
- Inc 1 st with Gray
- Inc 1 st with Light Blue

←Set asi
15 sts f
thumb

INSTRUCTIONS

Sizes: Women's (Men's)

MATERIALS

Yarn:

CYCA #1 (fingering), Baby Panda from Rauma (100% Merino wool, 191 yd/175 m / 50 g), Charcoal Gray 14: 50 (100) g

CYCA # (fingering), Cloud from Anzula (hand-dyed 80% Superwash Merino wool, 10% cashmere, 10% nylon, 575 yd/525 m / 100 g), Nimbus Cloud: 50 (100) g

Needles: U.S. size 0 (1.5) / 2 (2.5) mm, set of 5 dpn

Gauge: 40 (36) sts = 4 in / 10 cm.
Adjust needle size to obtain correct gauge if necessary.

Right Mitten

With Charcoal Gray, CO 80 sts. Divide sts over 4 dpn and join to work in the round. Work in k1, p1 ribbing as shown on the chart and then continue in St st.

Increase for the thumb gusset on each side of a center stitch as shown for a striped gusset. At dark line, set aside 15 thumb sts for the thumb (see page 15 for details).

Continue, shaping top of mitten as shown on chart (see page 13 for details). Cut yarn and draw end through rem sts; tighten.

Thumb

Pick up and knit 17 + 17 sts around thumbhole = 34 sts total (see page 15). Divide sts onto 4 dpn and work as shown on thumb chart. Cut yarn and draw end through rem sts; tighten.

Left Mitten

Work mirror-image from chart.

Finishing

Weave in all ends neatly on WS. Gently steam press under a damp pressing cloth to block.

Baby Mittens from Jæren

Once upon a time there was an empress named Léi Zŭ. One day she walked around the emperor's garden and then sat under a tree to drink a cup of tea. Suddenly a little round cocoon fell from the crown of the tree directly into her hot tea. As soon as it got wet, Léi Zŭ was able to draw off a very long and fine white thread.

This old Chinese story describes the discovery of silk, and specifically the methods that could be used to unwind silkworm cocoons into thread without breakage. This is supposed to have happened around 2700 BCE; and it is true that for the next 1500 years or so, China was the sole producer of high-quality silk. It was possible to make wild silk elsewhere, but it was always of much lower quality, because silkworms had to eat through the fibers to escape the cocoon.

Silk has always been a luxury fiber. Silken "night shirts" were one of the most exclusive garments around for a long time—and there's nowhere else in Europe with as many preserved night shirts as Norway. Eleven of them, as well as pieces of two more, are in Norwegian collections. These garments were probably knitted by professional handworkers in England or Germany. All of them feature purl stitch patterns worked on a stockinette background. Most of the patterns are eight-petaled roses. Several of them are also embellished with pretty embroidery.

There aren't very many old mittens to be found in Rogaland, but at the Jær Museum, there is a little child's mitten in light wool with a green twisted cord. I've reproduced it in a blend of fine alpaca and silk, and added a knitted cord.

When I grew up in the 1960s, it was normal to wear knitted clothes all winter. My mother was quite accomplished with her needles. This photo was taken in the winter of 1961-62.

I-Cord

1.

2.

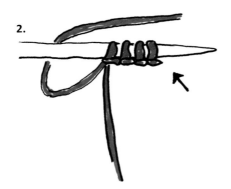

3.

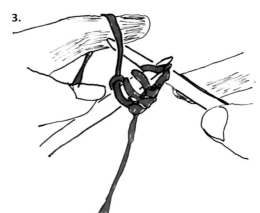

4.

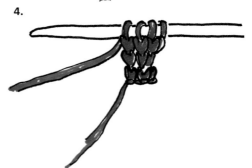

☐ Knit
☐ Twisted knit (knit through back loop)
v Purl
Yo, k2tog tbl

Chart 2

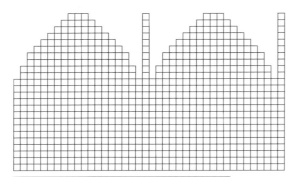

Chart 1

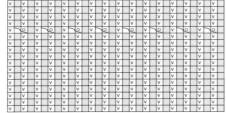

INSTRUCTIONS

Size: 6-9 months

MATERIALS
Yarn:
CYCA #2 (sport), Metalico from Blue Sky Fibers (50% alpaca, 50% silk, 147 yd/134 m / 50 g), Platinum 1612: 50 g

Needles: U.S. size 2.5 / 3 mm, set of 5 dpn

Gauge: 28 sts = 4 in / 10 cm.
Adjust needle size to obtain correct gauge if necessary.

Right Mitten
CO 32 sts. Divide sts over 4 dpn and join to work in the round. Following Chart 1, work around in k1tbl, p1 ribbing for 1¼ in / 3 cm. Next, make an eyelet round:
(K1tbl, yo, k2tog tbl, p1) around. Work 4 more rnds k1tbl, p1 ribbing.

Now, following Chart 2, continue in St st. On the first rnd, increase to 40 sts (inc 8 sts evenly spaced around). Work until mitten is 3¼ in / 8.5 cm long and then shape top.

Make sure there are 10 sts on each of the four needles before decreasing.

Rnd 1: *K1, ssk; knit until 3 sts rem on Needle 2, k2tog, k1*; rep * to * over Needles 3 and 4.
Rnd 2: Knit.
Repeat Rnds 1-2 two times and then decrease on every rnd. When 2 sts remain on each needle (8 sts total), cut yarn and draw end through rem sts; tighten.

Make the left mitten the same way.

Finishing
I-Cord: CO 3 sts. *Slide the sts back to needle tip, bring the yarn behind the work, tightening it as you move it from left to right, and k3*. Rep * to *. Make two cords, each about 14 in / 35 cm long.

Weave in all ends neatly on WS. Gently steam press under a damp pressing cloth to block. Draw cords through the eyelet rounds.

Vestland Rose

Knitting needles have been made with many different materials: bone and horn, various types of wood, iron, brass, and silver. For a long time, many people made their own needles. Later on, needles were produced with light metals and plastic. The newest ones are carbon. Knitting needles can be as thin as sewing needles or as thick as a person's little finger, depending on the intended use.

The finer the needles, the more stitches needed. With a large number of stitches, the options for patterning increase. For these mittens, I began with a well-known rose pattern and played a bit with the petal shapes. The result was an entirely new rose.

The cuffs on these mittens were inspired by an old pair of mittens from Voss. The technique of crossing stitches was well known in Fana, which is just outside Bergen. The oldest Fana sweaters were white and knitted in garter stitch. Some of them have a similar cable pattern around the edges of the body and sleeves.

INSTRUCTIONS

Sizes: Women's (Men's)

MATERIALS
Yarn:
CYCA #1 (fingering), Dale Babyull from Dale (100% wool, 180 yd/165 m / 50 g)

Yarn Amounts
Red 4018: 50 (100) g
Embroidery yarn from Setesdal Husflid, Pink: 50 (100) g (or use Dale Babyull, Shocking Pink 4516)

Needles: U.S. size 0 (1.5) / 2 (2.5) mm, set of 5 dpn; cable needle

Gauge: 34 (31) sts = 4 in / 10 cm.
Adjust needle size to obtain correct gauge if necessary.

Right Mitten
With Pink, CO 66 sts. Divide sts over 4 dpn and join to work in the round. Work the cuff following Chart 1. Rep the pattern a total of 4 times in length.

NOTE: The cables are worked from round to round so you will occasionally use sts from the previous and new rnds.

Fold the piece so the right side faces in.

Knit 1 rnd and, at the same time, decrease 4 sts evenly spaced around to 62 sts. Work around in St st with k1 Pink, k1 Red stripes. Continue the stripes until the lining and cuff are the same length—about 4½ in / 11.5 cm. Now continue as shown on Chart 2.

Increase for the thumb gusset as shown. At the dark line, set aside 12 thumb sts for the thumb (see page 15 for details).

Continue, shaping top of mitten as shown on chart (see page 13 for details). Cut yarn and draw end through rem sts; tighten.

Thumb
Pick up and knit 14 + 14 sts around thumbhole = 28 sts total (see page 15). Divide sts onto 4 dpn and work as shown on thumb chart. Shape and finish tip as for top of mitten.

Left Mitten
Work mirror-image from chart.

Finishing
Weave in all ends neatly on WS. Omitting the cuff, gently steam press under a damp pressing cloth to block. Fold the cuff up.

Thumb

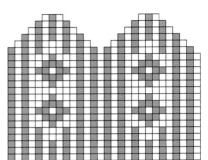

☐ Red—knit
▨ Pink—knit
▨ Pink—purl
◪ Sl 1 st to cable needle and hold behind work, p1, k1 from cable needle
◪ Sl 1 st to cable needle and hold in front of work, k1, p1 from cable needle

Chart 2

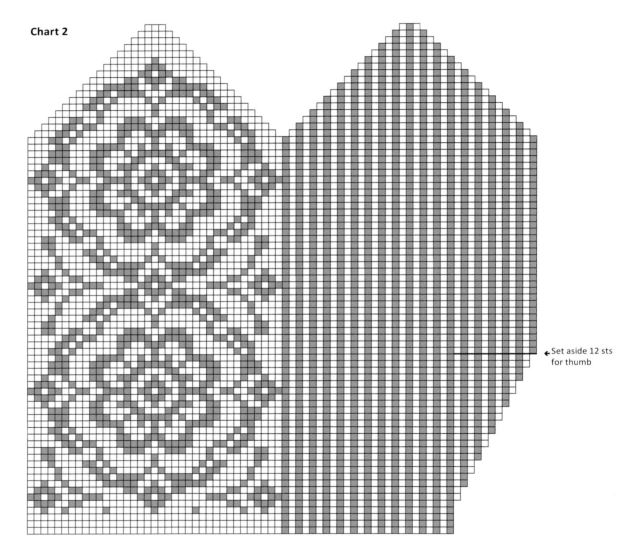

←Set aside 12 sts for thumb

Chart 1

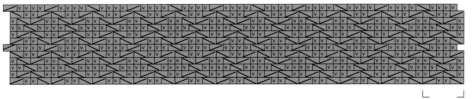

Pattern repeat

90

Mittens from Osterøy

A pair of well-preserved women's mittens were among the first items to become part of the Osterøy collections in 1922. They came from the tenant farm Kleivelandslia, of the farm Kleiveland on Osterøy. When Mikkjel Hansen Kleiveland (1839-1922) and his sister Kari died, the museum's antiquities department was invited to take anything of interest from the home.

Mikkjel and Kari were the children of Hans Mikkjelson Kleiveland (1806-1905) and Gunhild Johannesdatter Koppen (1794-1863). They married in 1834 and probably took over Kleivelandslia from his parents. Hans's father, Mikkjel Koppen, had gotten the place around 1804, a couple of years before Hans was born. The earnest money or "tenancy contract" was first arranged in 1852.

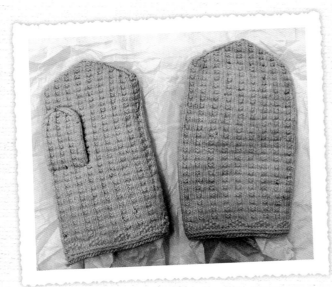

The houses on the land belonged to Hans and, by contract, he had the right to graze as many animals as the place could support. For upkeep and fuel, he could freely take stones and junipers. The rent was due twice a year and he did not have to perform any military service.

As far as tenant farmers go, Hans was unusual. He could both read and write. The museum has almanacs and notebooks in which he made notes on the weather and wind, harvests, and texts for the day. The historic collection at the University in Bergen was able to buy Hans's clothing in 1907. Among the items were a pair of wrist warmers and a pair of gloves.

When Hans died at the age of 99 years old, the farmer said the tenancy contract was terminated. This was difficult for Mikkjel and Kari, who were unmarried and had always lived at home, and were also advancing in years. They were able to move to the home of a relative in Koppen, and stayed there until their deaths.

The mittens most likely belonged to Kari and were probably used as church mittens. The original mittens were very short, so I decided to lengthen both the cuff and hand somewhat.

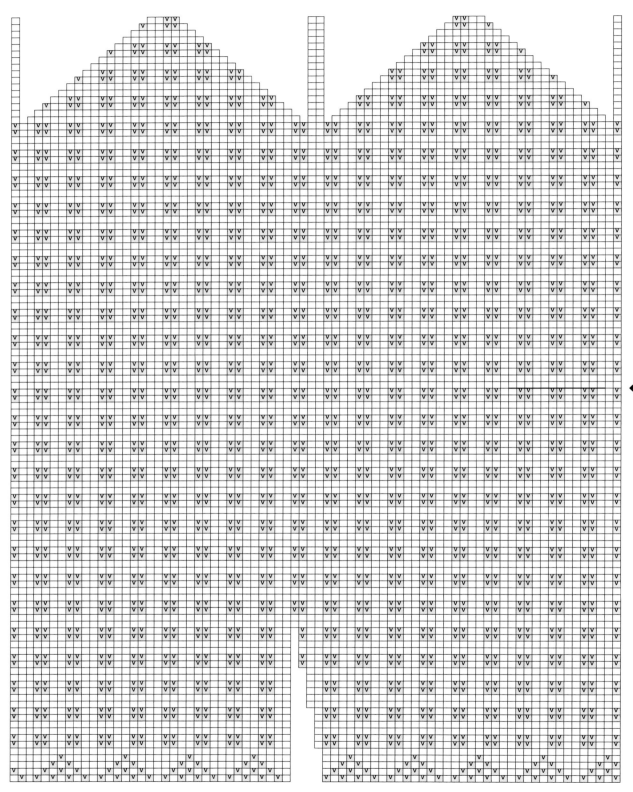

← Set aside 12
for the thum

Knit
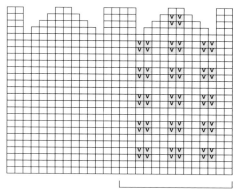 Purl

Thumb

Front of thumb

INSTRUCTIONS

Sizes: Women's (Men's)

MATERIALS

Yarn:
CYCA #1 (fingering), 2-ply Gammelserie from Rauma (100% wool, 175 yd/160 m / 50 g), Natural White 401: 100 (150) g

Needles: U.S. size 0 (1.5) / 2 (2.5) mm, set of 5 dpn

Gauge: 30 (27) sts in pattern = 4 in / 10 cm. Adjust needle size to obtain correct gauge if necessary.

Right Mitten
Holding two strands of yarn together, CO 72 sts with the long-tail method. Divide sts over 4 dpn and join to work in the round. Work 2 rnds of the two-end purl braid (see page 14) and then continue, following the chart. The increases at the side are worked at the same time as the knit/purl pattern.

Work following the chart to the dark line; set aside 12 thumb sts for the thumb (see page 15 for details).

Continue, shaping top of mitten as shown on chart (see page 13 for details). Cut yarn and draw end through rem sts; tighten.

Thumb
Pick up and knit 14 + 14 sts = 28 sts total around thumbhole (see page 15). Divide sts onto 4 dpn and work as shown on thumb chart. Cut yarn and draw end through rem sts; tighten.

Left Mitten
Work mirror-image from chart.

Finishing
Weave in all ends neatly on WS. Very gently steam press under a damp pressing cloth to block, making sure pattern is not flattened.

Ridged Mittens

Public 7-year school in Norway, also called "folk school," was established by law in 1889. At first, instruction only lasted for 12 weeks of the year in the countryside; but in the towns, the school session lasted for 40 weeks. The new law also positioned handwork and crafts as obligatory subjects.

The Women's Industry School in Kristiania was established with the mission to "awaken and spread the concepts of our national textile work." A three-month course for teachers was instituted in 1891. The goal was to create a unified method of hand-craft instruction for folk schools all around the country.

Sofie Borchgrevink (1846-1911), who had taken over as director of the Women's Industry School in 1888, was an accomplished leader. In a very short time, the school became a nationally recognized institution. She researched ideas in both Brussels and Paris. And it was she who wrote detailed teaching plans for each of the grades in folk schools. She also made sure new teachers had had the necessary introduction to the methodology.

Caroline Halvorsen (1853-1926) was responsible for these instructional programs. She taught at and directed the instructors' course at the school for more than 30 years—all the way until 1923. Halvorsen's Swedish mitten was recognized all around the country and was used as a model for the beginning classes. Both it and Halvorsen's stocking calculations were considered basic knowledge for young women.

Inspired by the easy mitten instructions in the *Knitting Book for Children's Schools and the Home*, published in 1901, I made a simple mitten that's elastic, warm, and fits well on the hand.

The boys had shop and the girls did handwork. Knitting was included in the time schedule for the handcraft hour at a school in Bergen—sometime between 1925 and 1935.

Thumb

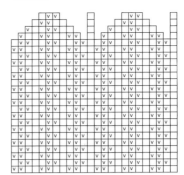

☐ White—knit
☑ White—purl
▨ Pink—knit
▨ Pink—purl

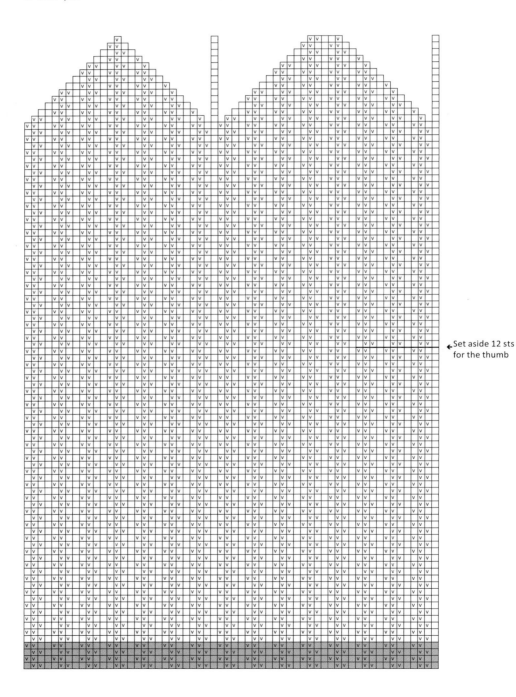

←Set aside 12 sts for the thumb

98

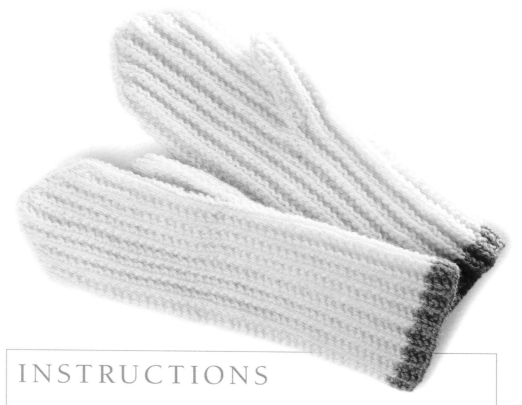

INSTRUCTIONS

Sizes: Women's (Men's)

MATERIALS
Yarn:
CYCA #2 (sport), PT5 from Rauma (100% wool, 140 yd/128 m / 50 g)

Yarn Amounts
Natural White 503: 50 (100) g
Pink 579: 50 (100) g

Needles: U.S. size 2.5 (4) / 3 (3.5) mm, set of 5 dpn

Gauge: 24 (22) sts = 4 in / 10 cm.
Adjust needle size to obtain correct gauge if necessary.

Right Mitten
With Pink, CO 60 sts. Divide sts over 4 dpn and join to work in the round. Work following the chart. The pattern is very easy: (K1, p2, k1) around. On the next rnd, shift the pattern 1 st to the left (= k2, p2) around. These 2 rounds are repeated throughout.

After two reps with Pink, change to Natural and continue in pattern until the mitten measures 5¼ in / 13 cm.

At the dark line, set aside 12 thumb sts on the right side for the thumb (see page 15 for

details). When the mitten is 8¼ / 21 cm long, begin shaping the top as follows: Divide the sts so there are 16 sts each on Needles 1 and 2 and 14 sts each on Needles 3 and 4. Work as described below or follow the chart.

Always knit the first st on Needle 1, ssk, and knit until 2 sts rem on Needle 2, k2tog. At beginning of Needle 3: K1, ssk, and knit until 2 sts rem on Needle 4, k2tog. Decrease the same way on every rnd until 3-3-1-1 sts rem. Cut yarn and draw end through rem sts; tighten.

Thumb
Pick up and knit 12 + 12 sts = 24 sts total around thumbhole (see page 15 for details). Divide sts onto 4 dpn and work as shown on thumb chart. Work in ridges as shown on the chart until thumb measures 2 in / 5 cm. With 6 sts on each needle, shape tip of thumb and finish as for top of mitten.

Left Mitten
Work as for right mitten but place the thumbhole at the left side.

Finishing
Weave in all ends neatly on WS. Very gently steam press under a damp pressing cloth to block, making sure pattern is not flattened.

Mittens from Sogn

Scattered all around Norway's museums, you'll find many lovely hand-carved winding sticks (*nøstepinner*). Inside there will be a loose ball that bounces around as the yarn is wound—making winding sticks almost as loud as baby rattles. It's said that this is intentional, so a housewife in another room could still tell whether a servant girl was doing her job.

The advantage of using a winding stick is that you can produce a yarn ball that allows yarn to be drawn from its center. That way, the yarn doesn't roll around. You can also knit from both ends of the yarn at the same time, using the end coming from the center of the ball and the end that's on the outside.

Textile tools were common lovers' gifts, and these items were often richly decorated—just like engagement mittens let a girl demonstrate her knitting skill, a gift like this let a boy demonstrate his woodworking ability. Carving out the loose ball was especially difficult, and was considered a labor of love.

This mitten was designed by Thora Gjerland, née Meel (1922-2012). She was an heiress from the estate of Meel in Vetlefjorden in Balestrand. She later married and lived in Leikanger. The mittens featured a design she knitted her whole life, for her children, children-in-law, and grandchildren. The mitten hand is narrow, which makes it fit well. She knitted shorter mittens without any stars for children.

Thora Gjerland with her children Astrid, Unni, and Per in 1959.

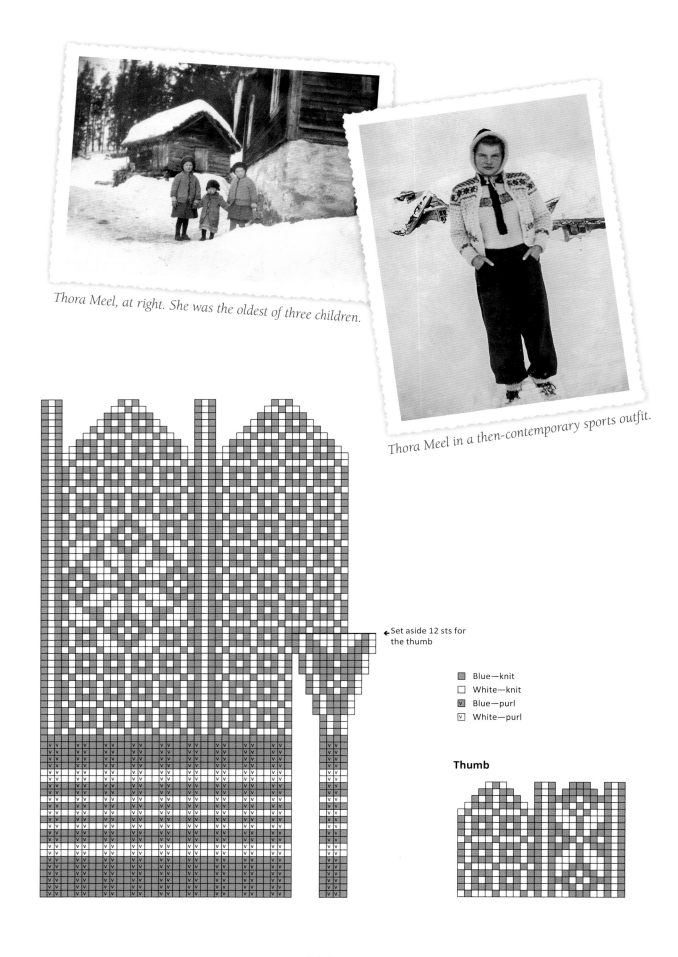

Thora Meel, at right. She was the oldest of three children.

Thora Meel in a then-contemporary sports outfit.

← Set aside 12 sts for the thumb

▨	Blue—knit
☐	White—knit
⊻	Blue—purl
⊽	White—purl

Thumb

INSTRUCTIONS

Sizes: Women's (Men's)

MATERIALS
Yarn:
CYCA #2 (sport), Ask / Hifa 2 from Hillesvåg (100% wool, 345 yd/315 m / 100 g)

Yarn Amounts
Navy Blue: 50 (100) g
Cream: 50 (100) g

Needles: U.S. size 4 (6) / 3.5 (4) mm, set of 5 dpn

Gauge: 24 (22) sts = 4 in / 10 cm.
Adjust needle size to obtain correct gauge if necessary.

Right Mitten
With Blue, CO 40 sts. Divide sts over 4 dpn and join to work in the round. Work following the chart, beginning with k2, p2 ribbing.

Continue in St st pattern, following the chart and increasing for the thumb gusset as shown. At the dark line, place 12 thumb sts on a holder. CO 8 sts over the gap. Continue as charted and shape top as shown (see page 13 for details). Cut yarn and draw end through rem sts; tighten.

Thumb
Pick up and knit 13 + 11 sts = 24 sts total around thumbhole. Divide sts onto 4 dpn and work as shown on thumb chart. Cut yarn and draw end through rem sts; tighten.

Left Mitten
Work mirror-image following the chart.

Finishing
Weave in all ends neatly on WS. Gently steam press under a damp pressing cloth to block.

Mittens from Sunnfjord

Sunnfjord Museum has two unique pairs of mittens and a half-finished mitten with a zigzag pattern that is noticeably different from other Norwegian mittens. The mittens are all a little different, but each was knitted back and forth until it was almost complete. The tip of the mitten was then knitted in the round on double-pointed needles at the same time as it was shaped. The thumb was worked separately and attached at the side, and then the mittens were seamed.

The museum curator thinks these mittens were made between 1880 and 1930. One pair, quite well-worn and darned, is from Lunde in Jølster. It's easy to believe that the other mittens came from the same village.

The thumbs on the old mittens aren't at exactly the same place—it was clearly difficult to match them when sewing them in. So I decided to knit the hand and thumb as one.

Where did the idea for these mittens come from? Both the shaping and the pattern are unique compared to other Norwegian mittens. The special zigzag pattern is worked back and forth. The thumb is knitted separately and then sewn on.

Thumb

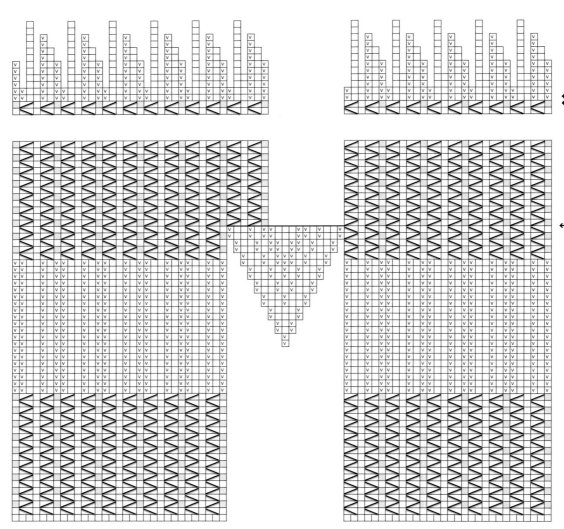

Front of thumb

☐   Knit on RS and purl on WS

ⓥ   Purl on RS and knit on WS

☐   Twisted knit = K1 tbl

◣   Knit the 2ⁿᵈ st from behind the 1ˢᵗ st without slipping either st off; knit 1ˢᵗ st and slip both sts from left needle.

◿   Purl the 2ⁿᵈ st going in front of the 1ˢᵗ st without slipping either st off; purl the 1ˢᵗ st and slip both sts from left needle.

← Divide the sts evenly onto 4 dpn and knit in the round while you shape the top.

← Continue until work measures 8¾ (9½) in / 22 (24) cm

← Set aside 17 sts for the thumb

INSTRUCTIONS

Sizes: Women's (Men's)

MATERIALS
Yarn:
CYCA #2 (sport), PT2 from Rauma (100% wool, 180 yd/165 m / 50 g), Lime-green 16: 100 (150) g

Needles: U.S. size 1.5 (2.5) / 2.5 (3) mm: straights and set of 5 dpn

Gauge: 21 (19) sts = 4 in / 10 cm.
Adjust needle size to obtain correct gauge if necessary.

Right and Left Mittens
Both mittens are worked the same way. With straight needles, CO 61 sts and work the zigzag pattern back and forth as described below. You don't need a cable needle.
Row 1: Purl.
Row 2: K1, *knit the 2nd st from behind the 1st st without slipping either st off; knit 1st st and slip both sts from left needle. K1, knit the 5th st from behind the 4th st, knit the 4th st and slip both sts from needle, p1*. Rep * to * across.
Row 3: K1tbl, *purl the 2nd st going in front of the 1st st without slipping either st off; purl the 1st st and slip both sts from left needle. P1, purl the 5th st going in front of the 4th st, purl the 4th st and slip both sts from needle, k1tbl*. Rep * to * across.
Rep Rows 2-3 until piece measures 2 in/ 5 cm.

Rib Row 1: P1, *k1, p1, k2, p2*. Rep * to * across.
Rib Row 2: *K2, p2, k1, p1*. Rep * to * across.

Continue as shown on the chart, increasing 17 sts for the thumb gusset (increase on each side of the center st). Place the thumb sts on a holder and then CO 6 sts over the gap.

When mitten measures 8¾ (9½) in / 22 (24) cm, divide the sts evenly onto 4 dpn. Join to work in the round and shape the top as shown on the chart. Cut yarn and draw end through rem sts; tighten.

Thumb
CO 7 sts and pick up and knit all 17 thumb sts from the holder. CO 1 more st and work following the thumb chart. When the section with the zigzag sts is complete, divide the sts evenly onto 4 dpn and join to work in the round. Shape tip as shown on chart. Cut yarn and draw end through rem sts; tighten.

Finishing
Seam the thumb and then attach it smoothly to the mitten hand. Graft each mitten at the side. Weave in all ends neatly on WS. Very gently steam press under a damp pressing cloth to block, making sure pattern is not flattened.

Children's Mittens from Nordfjord

The Nordfjord Museum's collection includes a special child's mitten in black and white wool. It's a left-hand mitten with a metal button sewn in at the top of the cuff. The museum received the mitten from the Holvik property in Sandane in 1982; there's no other information about it.

Mittens and stockings were knitted in the round on four or five needles. When knitting large garments in the round, up to 16 needles were sometimes used, until circular needles were invented at last—but we don't know exactly when. In 1881, a "circular fishbone needle" was described in the handcraft magazine *Dagmar* as "always being comfortable to knit with in the round." From the text we learn that readers probably already knew about this type of needle and had perhaps seen it at an aunt's or grandmother's house. These needles were also recommended for larger projects which were knitted flat, "because, with the round shaping of the needles, stitches wouldn't fall off the ends."

However, it's possible that familiarity with circular needles was limited to certain areas, because in the women's magazine *Urd* in 1925, the circular needle was presented as a new item. "It's so ridiculously simple and practical that it's peculiar that we've only just now thought of it."

The use of circular needles increased, and they became a standard tool for knitting sweaters and cardigans. The best-known brand in Norway was NOVI—circular needles were produced at the Novi Industry AS in Skedsmo starting around 1947.

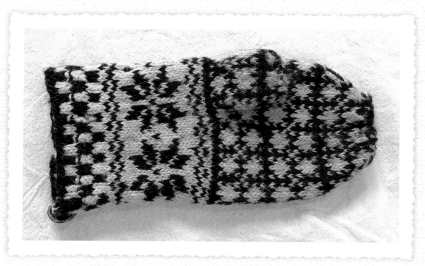

Many people call any black and white mitten a Selbu mitten. However, this small child's mitten doesn't have any of the characteristics typical of Selbu mittens. Black and white were the two most commonly available colors and were used for pattern knitting all over Norway. This mitten is well-constructed, with pattern bands that go all around the mitten.

Thumb

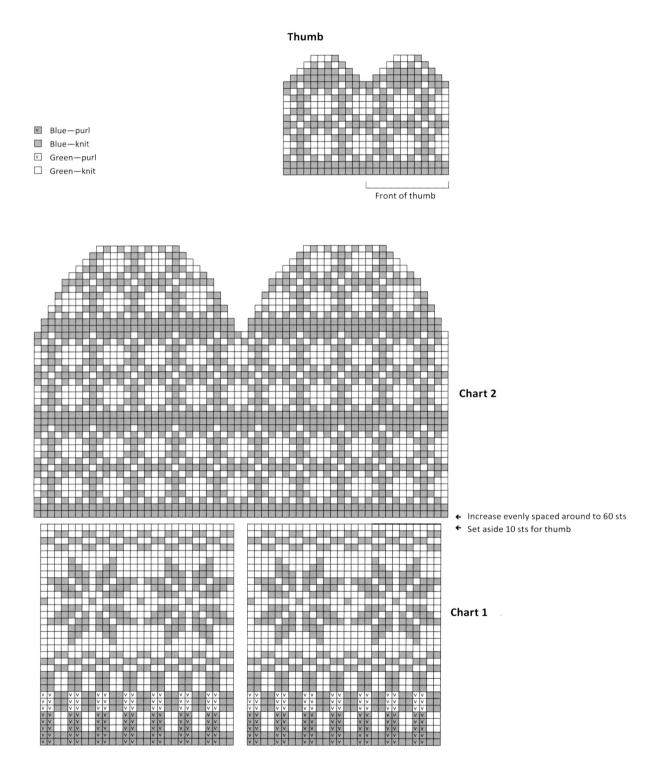

Blue—purl
Blue—knit
Green—purl
Green—knit

Front of thumb

Chart 2

← Increase evenly spaced around to 60 sts
← Set aside 10 sts for thumb

Chart 1

INSTRUCTIONS

Sizes: 4 (6, 8) years

MATERIALS
Yarn:
CYCA #2 (sport), PT5 from Rauma (80% wool, 20% polyamide, 140 yd/128 m / 50 g)

Yarn Amounts
Blue 567: 50 (50, 50) g
Light Green 582: 50 (50, 50) g

Needles: U.S. size 000 (0, 1.5) / 1.5 (2, 2.5) mm, set of 5 dpn

Gauge: 37 (36, 35) sts = 4 in / 10 cm. Adjust needle size to obtain correct gauge if necessary.

Right Mitten
With Blue, CO 56 sts. Divide sts over 4 dpn and join to work in the round. Work in k2, p2 ribbing following Chart 1. Continue in St st, setting aside 10 sts for the thumb (see page 15 for details) where indicated on the chart. Now increase 4 sts evenly spaced around to 60 sts. Following Chart 2, continue, shaping top of mitten as shown on chart (see page 13 for details). Graft the rem sts at top of mitten.

Thumb
Pick up and knit 12 + 12 sts around thumb-hole = 24 sts total (see page 15). Divide sts onto 4 dpn and work as shown on thumb chart. Cut yarn and draw end through rem sts; tighten.

Left Mitten
Work mirror-image from chart.

Finishing
Weave in all ends neatly on WS. Gently steam press under a damp pressing cloth to block.

Church Mittens from Nordfjord

The Nordfjord Folk Museum in Sandane has several mittens in its collection, including a pair of cabled wool mittens knit with fine white sheep's wool.

Norwegians were, of course, influenced by styles in Europe. Both lace and cables were popular. Many designs could be made by decreasing, increasing, with yarnovers, and by moving stitches. There are many mittens and especially half gloves knitted with white cotton in Norwegian museums, and these patterns are found all over the country. There might be edged blocks on the back of the hand or striped sections from the wrist to the fingertips.

Cotton was an expensive material, but garments of this type were also knitted in fine wool yarn. Some of these are wedding mittens while others are church mittens—accessories that were often more decorative than warm.

Much of this patterning is documented in Joanna Schreiner's book *Knitting Patterns from Great-Grandmother's Time*. It was published in 1911 and primarily featured lace patterns of various sorts. In the preface, she pointed out that these techniques had been much more widespread and that "now" (in 1911) they were almost gone. Among other patterns in the book, we find a design similar to those used for these mittens.

Various types of lace patterns were popular. This type of mitten was used for church on Sundays. This pretty pair knit in fine wool can be seen at the Nordfjord Folk Museum.

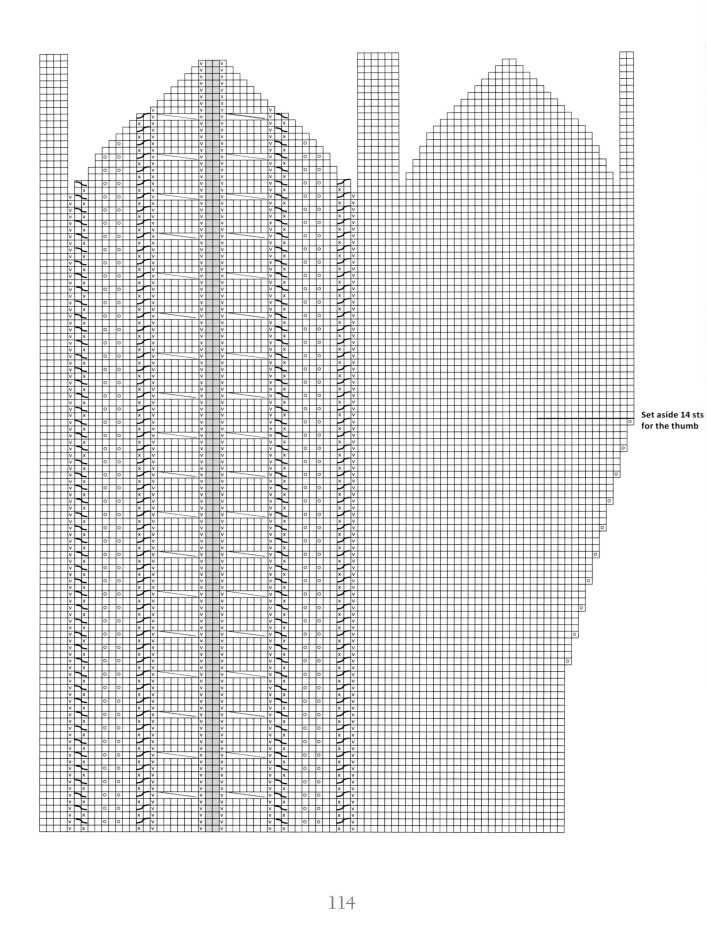

Set aside 14 sts
for the thumb

- ☐ Knit
- ☑ Purl
- ☐ Twisted knit = K1tbl
- ⊙ Yarnover
- ☒ No stitch
- ◹ K2tog
- ◸ K2tog tbl
- ▱ Sl 3 sts to a cable needle and hold in front of work, k3, k3 from cable needle

Thumb

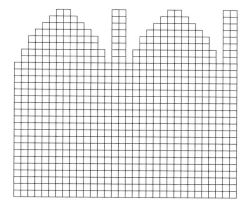

INSTRUCTIONS

Sizes: Women's (Men's)

MATERIALS
Yarn:
CYCA #2 (sport), Fine 2-ply Old Spelsau wool yarn from Selbu Spinneri (can be substituted with Ask / Hifa 2 from Hillesvåg) (100% wool, 345 yd/315 m / 100 g), White: 100 (150) g

Needles: U.S. size 0 (1.5) / 2 (2.5) mm, set of 5 dpn; cable needle

Gauge: 29 (26) sts = 4 in / 10 cm.
Adjust needle size to obtain correct gauge if necessary.

Right Mitten
CO 76 sts. Divide sts evenly over 4 dpn and join to work in the round. Knit 6 rnds. Next, work eyelet rnd for foldline: (k2tog, yo) around. Continue with cable and lace pattern on the back of the hand and St st on palm as shown on the chart. Increase for the thumb gusset with yarnovers as indicated on chart. At dark line, set aside 14 sts for thumb (see page 15 for details).

Shape top of mitten as shown on chart (see page 13 for details). Cut yarn and draw end through rem sts; tighten.

Thumb
Pick up and knit 16 + 16 sts = total of 32 sts (see page 15). Divide sts onto 4 dpn and work as shown on thumb chart. Cut yarn and draw end through rem sts; tighten.

Left Mitten
Work mirror-image from chart.

Finishing
Weave in all ends neatly on WS. Omitting all patterned areas, gently steam press under a damp pressing cloth to block.

Eternal Calendar Mittens

The 14th of October, the first day of winter, is marked on traditional calendar staffs with a mitten. This day was also called "moving day," because it was the day when servant contracts typically came into effect and new servants began work.

A calendar staff was an "eternal calendar" made of wood, with each day of the year carved in as a slash or notch. The staff had a summer side and a winter side. Every seventh day—the day of rest—was often well-highlighted. Holy days and special red letter days were marked with their own symbols. During the Catholic period, approximately every fourth day was a holy day. Each had its own symbol and was tied to weather predictions and important days for work life.

This kind of calendar was practical at a time when many people couldn't read, but it gradually fell out of use after the Gregorian calendar was established in 1700.

The mitten symbol is said to be in memory of the pope Calixtus, who suffered martyrdom in 222. Gloves, a cap, and a staff were often used as symbols for the clergy. In Norwegian folk tradition, mittens remind us that we are about to enter the colder season.

Several pairs of mittens and gloves from Midtre Gauldal have especially beautiful cuffs. I became so fascinated by these cuffs that I was inspired to play a little more with the possibilities that this technique presented.

Mittens from Budal, which today is part of Midtre Gauldal, marked with the date 1868. I think the cuffs on these hand garments are lovely, as well as fascinating.

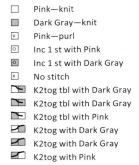

- ☐ Pink—knit
- ▨ Dark Gray—knit
- ⊻ Pink—purl
- ⊡ Inc 1 st with Pink
- ◉ Inc 1 st with Dark Gray
- ☒ No stitch
- ◤ K2tog tbl with Dark Gray
- ◤ K2tog tbl with Dark Gray
- ◤ K2tog tbl with Pink
- ◢ K2tog with Dark Gray
- ◢ K2tog with Dark Gray
- ◢ K2tog with Pink

Thumb

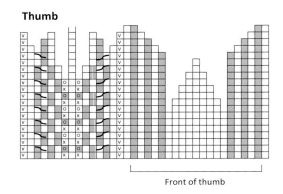

Front of thumb

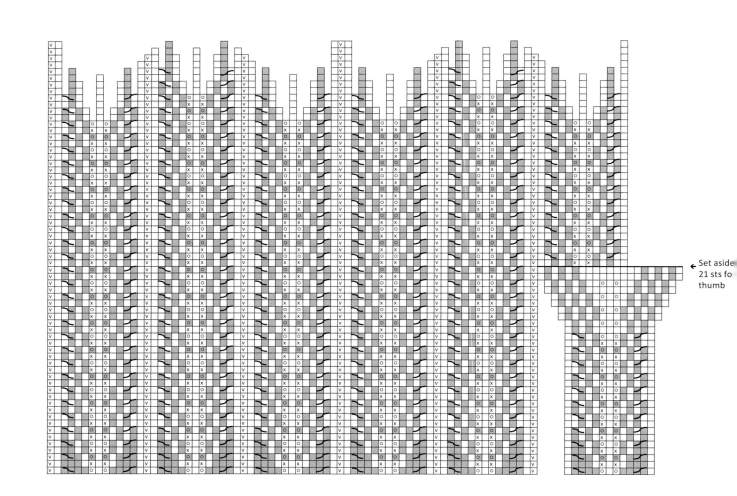

← Set aside
21 sts for
thumb

118

INSTRUCTIONS

Sizes: Women's (Men's)

MATERIALS
Yarn:
CYCA # 1 (fingering), Embroidery yarn from Setesdal Husflid, Pink: 100 (100) g
OR substitute CYCA #1 (fingering), Dale Baby Ull (100% wool, 180 yd/165 m / 50 g), Pink 4504 or Shocking Pink 4516: 50 (100) g
CYCA #3 (DK), Gotlandsk Pelsuld from Fil-colana (100% Gotland wool, 295 yd/270 m / 100 g), Gray 958: 100 (100) g

Needles: U.S. size 1.5 (2.5) / 2.5 (3) mm, set of 5 dpn
Crochet Hook: U.S. size C-2.5 (D-3) / 2.5 (3) mm

Gauge: 27 (25) sts = 4 in / 10 cm.
Adjust needle size to obtain correct gauge if necessary.

Right Mitten
With Pink, CO 72 sts. Divide sts evenly over 4 dpn and join to work in the round. Knit 1 rnd. Continue in charted pattern, increasing for the thumb gusset as shown. At the dark line, place 21 sts on a holder. CO 13 new sts over the gap and continue charted pattern. Shape the top as shown (see page 13 for details). Cut yarn and draw end through rem sts; tighten.

Thumb
Pick up and knit 21 + 15 sts = total of 36 sts and divide sts onto dpn. Knit the thumb as shown on thumb chart. Cut yarn and draw end through rem sts; tighten.

Ruffled Edge (can be omitted):
With Pink and RS facing, using a crochet hook if necessary, pick up and knit 72 sts around bottom edge of mitten.
Rnd 1: Knit.
Rnd 2: (K1, yo) around = 144 sts.
Rnd 3: Knit.
Rnd 4: Purl.
BO knitwise.

With Gray and WS facing, pick up and knit 72 sts in the first Pink rnd of edging.
Rnd 1: Knit.
Rnd 2: Knit.
Rnd 3: (K1, yo) around = 144 sts.
Rnd 4: Knit.
Rnd 5: Purl.
BO knitwise.

Left Mitten
Work mirror-image from chart.

Finishing
Weave in all ends neatly on WS.
Omitting the ruffled edge, gently steam press under a damp pressing cloth to block.

Mittens from Surnadal

In conjunction with a large knitting exhibition in 1984, the Romsdal Museum registered a man's mitten from Surnadal. It was knitted in fine black and white yarn, probably handspun. The same motif is repeated, and it doesn't look like there were any increases for a thumb gusset. The initials CIS are knitted in. A short ribbed cuff of much finer yarn was knitted on later.

The same basic pattern was also found in Viksdalen in Gaular—a little further south, in Vestland. A pair of mittens in the collection of the University Museum in Bergen was knitted for a wedding in 1909. The bride knitted two pairs so she and her bridegroom would have matching mittens. According to her son, she had some older knitted garments with the same pattern that she could study.

The Viksdal mittens are red and black with striated ribbing, while the stripes on the ribbing of the Surnadal mittens run in the opposite direction. I decided to omit the ribbing altogether.

This mitten didn't originally have a ribbed cuff. The striped edging was later knitted on with a considerably finer yarn.

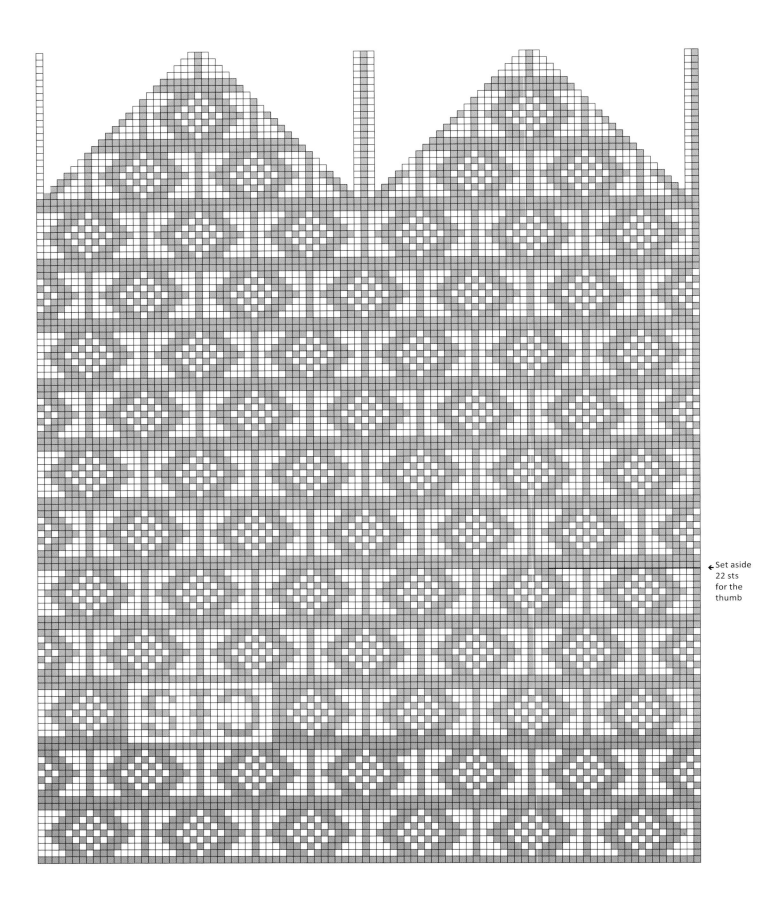

Set aside 22 sts for the thumb

Thumb

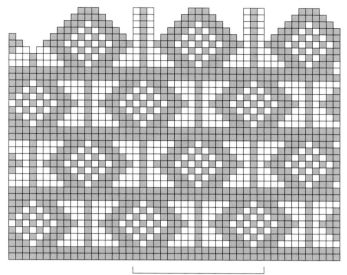

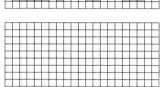

Front of thumb

☐ White—knit
▧ Purple—knit

INSTRUCTIONS

Sizes: Women's (Men's)

MATERIALS
Yarn:
CYCA #1 (fingering), Lanett Babyull Super-wash from SandnesGarn (100% Merino wool, 191 yd/175 m / 50 g), Purple 4855: 50 (100) g
CYCA #1 (fingering) 2-ply Spelsau Strikkegarn (100% wool, 244 yd/ 223 m / 50 g), Natural White: 50 (100) g

Needles: U.S. size 000 (0) / 1.5 (2) mm, set of 5 dpn

Gauge: 42 (38) sts = 4 in / 10 cm.
Adjust needle size to obtain correct gauge if necessary.

Right Mitten
With White over thumb and Purple over index finger, use the long-tail method to CO 96 sts. Knit 4 rows (= 2 ridges) back and forth. Divide sts over 4 dpn and join to work in the round. Work in St st following the

chart. On one of the mittens, I added the original initials and on the other, the year knitted. You can, of course, substitute your own initials or omit them altogether. At the dark line, set aside 22 sts for the thumb (see page 15 for details). Shape top as shown on chart (see page 13 for details). Cut yarn and draw end through rem sts; tighten.

Thumb
Pick up and knit 24 + 24 sts = 48 sts total around thumbhole (see page 15). Divide sts onto 4 dpn and work as shown on thumb chart. Cut yarn and draw end through rem sts; tighten.

Left Mitten
Work mirror-image following the chart.

Finishing
Weave in all ends neatly on WS. Gently steam press under a damp pressing cloth to block.

Aasta Mittens

This pair of mittens is named for my good friend Aasta Olstad, who was born in Røtvei in 1928 and grew up on her grandparents' farm in Oppdal. They had a number of animals, including sheep. Her grandmother spun yarn and wove fabric. At an early age, Aasta and her sister, Eli, who was a year younger, had to learn to card wool. It was hard work all winter for such small girls. During the summers, they knitted when they were at the summer pasture. Both girls had to make whatever they needed in terms of mittens and socks. To sit without any work in your hands just wasn't allowed.

Aasta remembers that mittens were knitted rather large. Mittens for everyday use were felted to make them warmer and stronger, using salt water. The mittens were usually a single color, sheep's white or sheep's black. Occasionally, they put some stripes in the ribbing. For more formal occasions, they had pattern-knitted mittens.

It's likely that their days were the same as those for many young girls before the war. There was very little money for buying clothes and shoes, and most things were homemade. Textile work takes a lot of time, so everyone had to contribute in every way they could.

The pattern panels on these cuffs were inspired by the decorative edge of an old glove.

A photo from Vollan School in Oppdal about 1938. Aasta and Eli Røtvei (numbers three and four from the left) wore school aprons to protect their clothing. On their hands, you can see the thick wool mittens they knitted themselves while at the summer pasture. Homemade "devil's" caps were the height of fashion. On their legs, they're wearing wool socks and roomy ski boots to grow into. Aasta had only one ski when the school photo was taken; the other one had broken.

Thumb

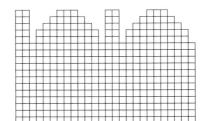

- ▣ Pink—knit
- ⱴ Pink—purl
- ☐ Natural White—knit
- ⱴ Natural White—purl
- ⊡ Inc 1 st knitwise

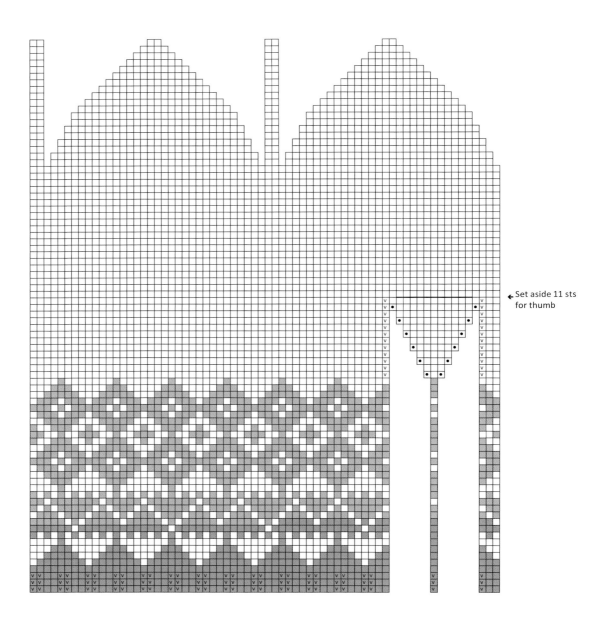

← Set aside 11 sts for thumb

INSTRUCTIONS

Sizes: Women's (Men's)

MATERIALS
Yarn:
CYCA #3 (DK), Sterk from Du Store Alpakka (40% Merino wool, 40% alpaca, 20% poly-amide, 150 yd/137 m / 50 g), Natural White 806: 100 (100) g
CYCA #2 (sport), Arroyo from Malabrigo (100% Merino wool, 335 yd/ 306 m / 100 g), English Rose 057: 50 g

Needles: U.S. size 2.5 (4) / 3 (3.5) mm, set of 5 dpn

Gauge: 25 (22) sts = 4 in / 10 cm.
Adjust needle size to obtain correct gauge if necessary.

Right Mitten
With Pink, CO 56 sts. Divide sts over 4 dpn and join to work in the round. Work around in k2, p2 ribbing as shown on chart. Continue in color pattern and St st following the chart. When the cuff is complete, begin thumb gusset, increasing as shown. Note that the st on each side of the gusset is purled. At the dark line, set aside 11 sts for the thumb (see page 15 for details). Shape top as shown on chart (see page 13 for details). Cut yarn and draw end through rem sts; tighten.

Thumb
Pick up and knit 13 + 13 sts = 26 sts total around thumbhole (see page 15). Divide sts onto 4 dpn and work as shown on thumb chart. Cut yarn and draw end through rem sts; tighten.

Left Mitten
Work mirror-image following the chart.

Finishing
Weave in all ends neatly on WS. Gently steam press under a damp pressing cloth to block.

Selbu Mittens with "Six-Petaled Roses"

My mother had two pairs of unused Selbu mittens in the bottom of a chest. She might be the one who knitted them, or they might have been knitted in Selbu.

I found a pattern for one of the pairs in *Every Woman's Knitting Book* from 1940. The *Every Woman's Knitting* magazine began publishing two years earlier and, at that time, knitting patterns were an essential part of the contents. Motifs and pattern instructions were especially important during the war. If the patterns were for "experienced knitters," it was emphasized in the title. Mittens could be knitted with rose-patterned cuffs or striped ribbing. "The prettiest are, without a doubt, rose panels," according to the text.

The typical Selbu mitten consists of a mitten "leaf" with a cuff (*vekk* is the local word)— which is to say, with a ribbing or decorative finish. The front and back sides of the mitten "leaf" had different motifs. In between was a vertical stripe. The thumb also had a front and back with different motifs and the vertical stripe in between.

Another characteristic of Selbu mittens is the marked difference between men's and women's mittens—something very few of us reflect on today. As the Selbu regional curator Birgitta Odén points out, "Men's mittens have patterns on the entire cuff with only 2-3 rounds of purl and knit stitches. Women's mittens have a long cuff; usually ribbed, but a chevron or lace cuff was also common."

Knitting mittens and socks was part of daily life for anyone above school age in Selbu. It brought in welcome income. Here we see a tailor, Kristen Jørgensen Lien, swinging the needles. He was born on November 12, 1862, and was 84 years old when this photo was taken in 1947.

Chart 2

← Set aside 15 sts for thumb

Chart 1

Thumb

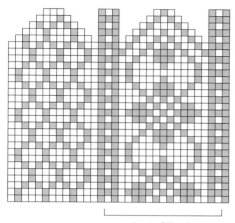

Front of thumb

☐ White—knit
▦ Black—knit
▣ Inc 1 st with Black

INSTRUCTIONS

Sizes: Women's (Men's)

MATERIALS
Yarn:
CYCA #1 (fingering), Gammelserie from
Rauma (100% wool, 175 yd/160 m / 50 g)

Yarn Amounts
Black 436: 50 (100) g
White 400: 50 (100) g

Needles: U.S. size 000 (0) / 1.5 (2) mm, set
of 5 dpn

Gauge: 35 (32) sts = 4 in / 10 cm.
Adjust needle size to obtain correct gauge
if necessary.

Version 1
Striped Ribbing:
With Black, CO 60 sts. Divide sts over 4 dpn
and join to work in the round. Work 4 rnds k2,
p2 ribbing. Continue in ribbing, alternating 2
rnds White and 2 rnds Black until there are a
total of 6 White stripes. End with 4 rnds Black.

Version 2
Patterned Cuff:
With White, CO 60 sts. Divide sts over 4 dpn

and join to work in the round. Work 4 rnds
k1, p1 ribbing. Continue in St st, following
Chart 1.

Right Mitten
When the cuff is complete, continue on to
Chart 2. Increase for the thumb gusset as
shown. At the dark line, place 15 sts on a
holder for the thumb. CO 14 sts over the
gap and continue following the chart.
Shape top as shown on chart (see page
13 for details). Cut yarn and draw end
through rem sts; tighten.

Thumb
Pick up and knit 17 + 15 sts = 32 sts total
around thumbhole. Divide sts onto 4 dpn
and work as shown on thumb chart. Cut yarn
and draw end through rem sts; tighten.

Left Mitten
Work mirror-image following the chart.

Finishing
Weave in all ends neatly on WS.
Gently steam press under a damp
pressing cloth to block.

Selbu Mittens with a Flower Border

The other pair of mittens in my mother's chest was a pair of man's mittens. The short cuff with pattern-knitted embellishment encircling the cuff is typical for men's mittens from Selbu. These are decorated with what the locals call "flowers."

The various pattern elements used in Selbu have special names. "Weathervane rose," *tellros* (counting rose), and "orange," for example. *Værhåinn* is the local word for a weathervane and refers to the hooked points of the vanes. *Storhåen* ("big H") has a crossbar similar to the letter H. The common eight-petaled rose is called *skjænnrosa* or *sjænnrosa*. In addition, the names sometimes indicate how big the motif is. Whether the patterns have 4 or 6 stitches in the petals determines whether they're called four-petaled or six-petaled roses.

Spelsau sheep have both long, lustrous, wavy outercoat hair to protect them against wind and weather and an undercoat of short fine wool to keep them warm. This knitting motif is called the "weathervane rose" because it's inspired by the vanes of a weathervane.

Thumb

☐ White—knit
▨ Black—knit

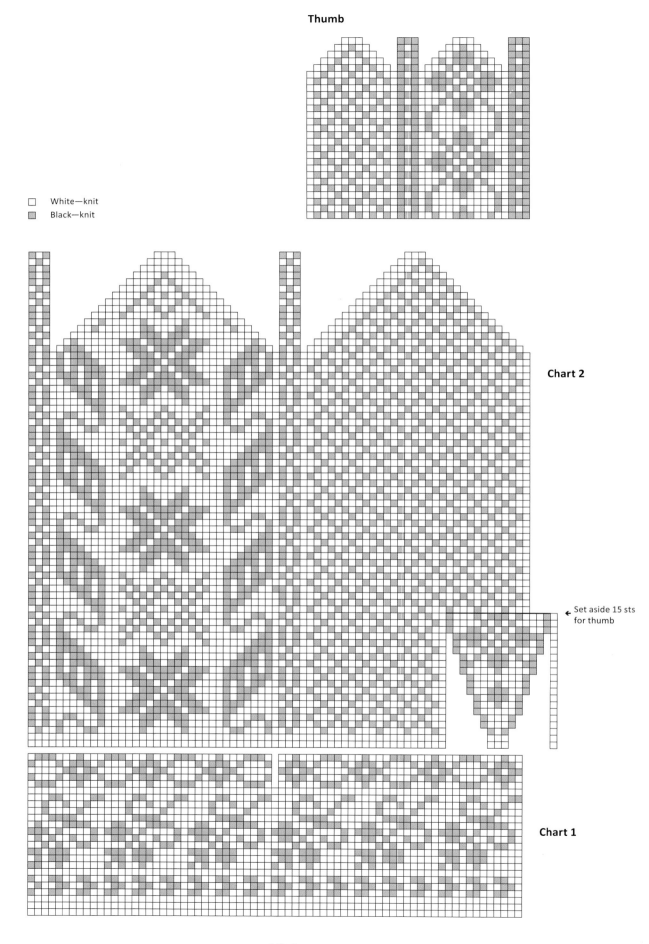

Chart 2

← Set aside 15 sts
for thumb

Chart 1

134

INSTRUCTIONS

Sizes: Women's (Men's)

MATERIALS
Yarn:
CYCA #1 (fingering), Gammelserie from Rauma (100% wool, 175 yd/160 m / 50 g)

Yarn Amounts
Black 436: 50 (100) g
White 400: 50 (100) g

Needles: U.S. size 2.5 (4) / 3 (3.5) mm, set of 5 dpn

Gauge: 31 (28) sts = 4 in / 10 cm.
Adjust needle size to obtain correct gauge if necessary.

Right Mitten
With White, CO 72 sts. Divide sts over 4 dpn and join to work in the round. Work 3 rnds k2, p2 ribbing and then continue in St st until piece measures 2½ in / 6 cm. Purl 1 rnd (foldline) and then work following Chart 1.
NOTE: On Rnd 20, dec 1 st at center as indicated on the chart.

After completing cuff (Chart 1), dec evenly spaced around to 64 sts. Now work following Chart 2.

Increase for the thumb gusset as shown. At the dark line, place 15 sts on a holder for the thumb. CO 12 sts over the gap and continue following the chart. Shape top as shown on chart (see page 13 for details). Cut yarn and draw end through rem sts; tighten.

Thumb
Pick up and knit 16 + 16 sts = 32 sts total around thumbhole. Divide sts onto 4 dpn and work as shown on thumb chart. Cut yarn and draw end through rem sts; tighten.

Left Mitten
Work mirror-image following the chart.

Finishing
Weave in all ends neatly on WS. Fold the cuff under at the foldline and loosely sew down edge on WS. Gently steam press under a damp pressing cloth to block.

Women's Mittens with "Weathervane Roses"

Today, there are few of us who could knit a pair of Selbu mittens without pattern instructions. In her thesis and doctoral work, Janne Reitan points out that what distinguished traditional Selbu knitting from other types of knitting was that knitters didn't use a pattern ready-made by designers. Experienced knitters arranged their own designs and adjusted them to the shaping of the items to be knitted. The motifs had to fit within the decrease lines on both the mitten hand and thumb. However, this method was used before there was a strong tradition of written and unwritten rules.

Knitters also designed while they were knitting. They learned pattern motifs from others or created new ones, which eventually became part of the traditional framework. This both allowed and challenged knitters to create new and different patterns every single time, according to Reitan. She calls it improvisation before tradition.

Inspired by this method of working, I designed my own Selbu mittens. The pattern elements were taken from old mittens and gloves. The cuffs are long—as they often used to be on women's mittens. (This might be because women wore shawls rather than jackets outdoors. Long cuffs helped keep their arms from freezing.)

Thumb

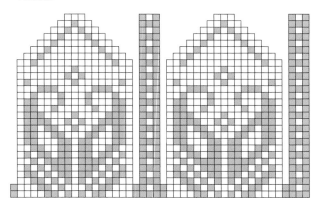

☐ White—knit
▨ Black—knit
⊡ Inc 1 knitwise
▣ Inc 1 knitwise with Black

← Set aside 20 sts
  for thumb

138

INSTRUCTIONS

Sizes: Women's (Men's)

MATERIALS
Yarn:
CYCA #1 (fingering), Gammelserie from Rauma (100% wool, 175 yd/160 m / 50 g)

Yarn Amounts
Black 436: 100 (100) g
White 401: 100 (100) g

Needles: U.S. size 0 (1.5) / 2 (2.5) mm, set of 5 dpn

Gauge: 34 (31) sts = 4 in / 10 cm.
Adjust needle size to obtain correct gauge if necessary.

Right Mitten
With White, CO 60 sts. Divide sts over 4 dpn and join to work in the round. Work the lace chevron pattern as follows:
Rnd 1: *K2tog, k2, yo, k1, yo, k2, ssk, p1, k1, p1*; rep * to * around.

Rnd 2: *K9, p1, k1, p1*. Rep * to * around.
Rep these 2 rnds in the following stripe sequence:
**10 rnds White
1 rnd Black
1 rnd White
2 rnds Black
1 rnd White
1 rnd Black
1 rnd White
2 rnds Black
1 rnd White
1 rnd Black**
Rep from ** to ** 2 times.
End with 10 rnds White.

After completing lace chevron section of cuff, continue, following the chart. If you want a regular length for the mitten, or you are working the Men's size, you can omit the horizontal vine pattern.

Increase for the thumb gusset as shown. At the dark line, set aside 20 sts for the thumb (see page 15 for details). CO 12 sts over the gap and continue following the chart. Shape top as shown on chart (see page 13 for details). Cut yarn and draw end through rem sts; tighten.

Thumb
Pick up and knit 22 + 22 sts = 44 sts total around thumbhole (see page 15). Divide sts onto 4 dpn and work as shown on thumb chart. Cut yarn and draw end through rem sts; tighten.

Left Mitten
Work the lace chevron and vine pattern as for right mitten. Work the rest of the mitten mirror-image following the chart.

Finishing
Weave in all ends neatly on WS. Gently steam press under a damp pressing cloth to block.

Child's Mittens from Selbu

Ever since Norway was Christianized, baptism has been a very important ceremony. In the Middle Ages there was a severe punishment for postponing a child's baptism longer than absolutely necessary. In Norwegian law in 1687, the deadline was eight days after the birth. This deadline was no longer official at the end of the eighteenth century, but even in the nineteenth century, children were expected to have been baptized no later than three days after birth.

In 1953, the school inspector Johannes Dahl in North-Trøndelag wrote that "[i]n the old days, people greatly feared that children might die before they were baptized. To die without baptism, they believed, meant the child would not be saved. Those who lived far away and for whom it was difficult to go to the church with their small children, especially in the winter, had permission to perform the baptism at home. When weather and conditions improved, they could go to church to have the baptism registered."

Children were dressed in the most elegant clothing possible for baptism. Long white dresses for both boys and girls are the most common outfit today. Earlier, the outfits were much more colorful.

If children went outside in the winter, they also needed mittens. This pair of mittens is knitted much like a pair at the Selbu Municipal Museum—perhaps they were baptism mittens. The originals were knitted with fine white and red wool yarn. I allowed myself to substitute a mixture of pink silk and silver thread for the red.

The Selbu town museum has a pair of small child's mittens in red and white on display. It wasn't uncommon to knit mittens for special occasions—perhaps these are baptism mittens.

Thumb

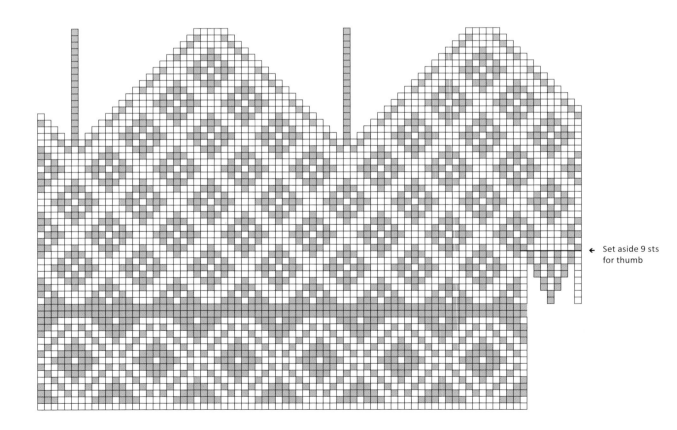

front of thumb

← Set aside 9 sts
for thumb

INSTRUCTIONS

Sizes: 6 months-1 year (2 years)

MATERIALS
Yarn:
CYCA #2 (sport), Fine 2-ply Old Spelsau wool yarn from Selbu Spinneri (can be substituted with Ask / Hifa 2 from Hillesvåg) (100% wool, 345 yd/315 m / 100 g), White: 50 g
CYCA #3 (DK), Rhapsody Glitter Light from Artyarns (85% mohair, 15% silk, 400 yd/366 m / 80 g), Pink with silver thread H1: 25 g

Needles: U.S. size 000 (0) / 1.5 (2) mm, set of 5 dpn

Gauge: 44 (42) sts = 4 in / 10 cm.
Adjust needle size to obtain correct gauge if necessary.

Right Mitten
With one strand of each color, use long-tail method to CO 72 sts. Divide sts evenly over 4 dpn and join to work in the round. Work 1 rnd of two-end purl braid (see page 14) and then continue in St st following the chart. Increase for the thumb gusset as indicated on chart. At dark line, set aside 9 sts for thumb (see page 15 for details).
Shape top of mitten as shown on chart. Cut yarn and draw end through rem sts; tighten.

Thumb
Pick up and knit 11 + 11 sts = total of 22 sts (see page 15). Divide sts onto 4 dpn and knit the thumb as shown on thumb chart. Cut yarn and draw end through rem sts; tighten.

Left Mitten
Work mirror-image from chart.

Finishing
To keep the mitten on the child, twist a little cord with white yarn and sew cord securely to the side opposite the thumb on each mitten. Weave in all ends neatly on WS. Gently steam press under a damp pressing cloth to block.

The Folk Museum's Selbu Mittens

The Norwegian Folk Museum in Oslo has several Selbu mittens. About this pair, it says "Brukssted: Selbu." It also states that the mittens were transferred from the Art Industry Museum in 1955.

The pattern is not typical for Selbu. On the other hand, the pair could have been knitted before it was usual to knit for sale. By the 1870s, two-color stranded knitting was already distinctive in Selbu. The parish priest Ole Stuevold-Hansen wrote in 1873 that "[t]he Selbu girls are masters at knitting artfully. They have their own type of knitting called 'two-strand socks' and 'two-strand mittens' with spades and diamonds, roses and stars all over." Two years later, Oscar Tybring described them this way: "They are so accomplished at knitting stockings and mittens with all kinds of figures and flourishes."

Early on, the mittens became marketable goods outside the local area. The popularity of skiing in both Norway and Europe contributed to high demand for Selbu mittens. Between the wars, everyone between the ages of 5 and 85 knitted, and the mittens provided income in wartime. However, great demand and high production quickly led to lowered quality. Knitters were paid per pair, which meant they earned more by knitting loosely on big needles with thick yarn. If stitches were dropped, they seldom had time to pick them up, and patterns were less precisely worked. Fortunately, these issues were recognized and in 1934 the Selbu Handicrafts Central was established. After that, standards that everyone had to follow were introduced. Official motifs were charted and distributed to knitters—which is why some of the patterns are better known than others.

Thumb

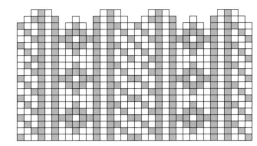

← Set as
15 sts
thumb

146

INSTRUCTIONS

Sizes: Women's (Men's)

MATERIALS
Yarn:
CYCA #1 (fingering), Babyull from Dale (100% Merino wool, 180 yd/165 m / 50 g), Blue 5545: 50 (100) g
CYCA #1 (fingering), Lanett Babyull Superwash from Sandnes Garn (100% Merino Wool, 191 yd/175 m / 50 g), Gray 1032: 50 (100) g

Needles: U.S. size 0 (1.5) / 2 (2.5) mm, set of 5 dpn

Gauge: 37 (34) sts = 4 in / 10 cm. Adjust needle size to obtain correct gauge if necessary.

Right Mitten
With Blue, CO 80 sts. Divide sts over 4 dpn and join to work in the round. Work in St st for 3/8 in / 1 cm. Purl 1 rnd for foldline and

then continue, following the chart. Increase for the thumb gusset as shown. At the dark line, set aside 15 sts for the thumb (see page 15 for details). Continue following the chart. Shape top as shown on chart. Cut yarn and draw end through rem sts; tighten.

Thumb
Pick up and knit 17 + 17 sts = 34 sts total around thumbhole. Divide sts onto 4 dpn and work in pattern as shown on thumb chart. Cut yarn and draw end through rem sts; tighten.

Left Mitten
Work mirror-image following the chart.

Finishing
Weave in all ends neatly on WS. Fold the cuff under at the foldline and loosely sew down edge on WS. Gently steam press under a damp pressing cloth to block.

Mittens from Gauldal

During the fieldwork undertaken by the Norwegian Folk Museum in Budalen in Midtre Gauldal in 1987, a pair of mittens from Bjerenås was photographed. The pattern consists of simple diamond blocks in black and gray covering the entire mitten. There is a cross inside each block and the thumb was knitted in a typical fishbone pattern. The mittens have several features in common with a pair of mittens from the same district that date to 1868.

I reconstructed the mittens from the photograph but decided to make a few small changes. Among other things, I knitted the cuff separately and then joined it to the mitten afterwards to prevent it from rolling up.

The pattern on these mittens encircles the whole hand. The upturned cuff at the lower edge is typical for men's mittens in that district.

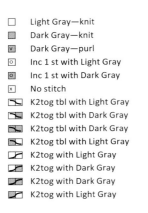

☐ Light Gray—knit

▨ Dark Gray—knit

▼ Dark Gray—purl

⊡ Inc 1 st with Light Gray

⊙ Inc 1 st with Dark Gray

☒ No stitch

⊱ K2tog tbl with Light Gray

⊱ K2tog tbl with Dark Gray

⊱ K2tog tbl with Dark Gray

⊱ K2tog tbl with Light Gray

⊰ K2tog with Light Gray

⊰ K2tog with Dark Gray

⊰ K2tog with Dark Gray

⊰ K2tog with Light Gray

Thumb

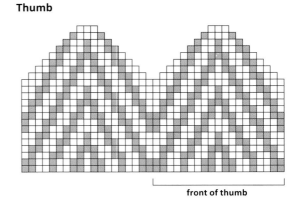

front of thumb

Chart 2

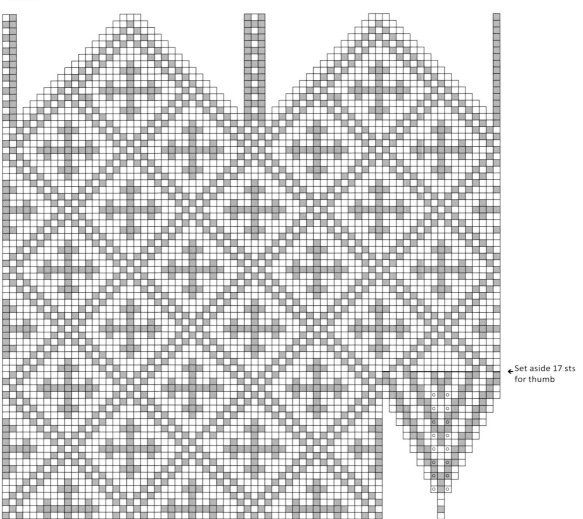

←Set aside 17 sts for thumb

Chart 1

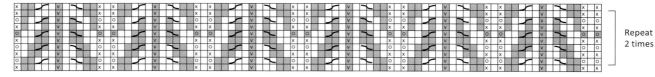

Repeat 2 times

INSTRUCTIONS

Sizes: Women's (Men's)

MATERIALS
Yarn:
CYCA #2 (sport), Mohair by Canard (65% mohair, 35% Merino wool, 193 yd/176 m / 50 g)

Yarn Amounts
Dark Gray 2101: 50 (100) g
Light Gray 2102: 50 (100) g

Needles: U.S. size 1.5 (2.5) / 2.5 (3) mm, set of 5 dpn

Gauge: 31 (28) sts = 4 in / 10 cm.
Adjust needle size to obtain correct gauge if necessary.

Right Mitten
With Dark Gray, CO 56 sts. Divide sts over 4 dpn and join to work in the round. Work 6 rnds in St st and then continue in pattern on Chart 2. Increase for thumb gusset as shown, increasing on each side of a center st. At the dark line, set aside 17 sts for the thumb (see page 15 for details). Continue following the chart. Shape top as shown on chart (see page 13 for details on shaping). Cut yarn and draw end through rem sts; tighten.

Thumb
Pick up and knit 19 + 19 sts = 38 sts total around thumbhole. Divide sts onto 4 dpn and work in pattern as shown on thumb chart. Cut yarn and draw end through rem sts; tighten.

Cuff
With Light Gray, CO 72 sts. Divide sts over 4 dpn and join to work in the round. Work in pattern as shown on Chart 1. After completing the last rnd, 60 sts rem. Dec another 4 sts evenly spaced around = 56 sts rem.

Joining Mitten and Cuff
Pick up and knit 56 sts around edge of mitten and divide sts onto 4 dpn with 14 sts on each needle. Divide the sts on the cuff so there are also 14 sts on each of the 4 dpn. Place the cuff outside the mitten. Make sure that the center of the repeat is aligned with the center of the mitten. Join the cuff and mitten by working three-needle bind-off around. *Three-needle bind-off:* K2tog (with 1 st from each needle), *k2tog; pass 1st st on right needle over 2nd; rep from * until all sts have been bound off.

Left Mitten
Work mirror-image following the chart.

Finishing
Weave in all ends neatly on WS. Pin out mittens, pinning out cuffs so that gentle waves follow the pattern. Sprinkle well with water and leave to dry for at least 24 hours.

Krus Mittens from Røros

One type of mittens, pictured and discussed in Ingeborg Gravjord's book *Mittens in the Norwegian Tradition*, is called *krus* mittens. They come from Mikkelssgården at Feragen, where the owner lived between 1851 and 1947. The initials AAS are knitted in. The pair was knitted with red and black yarn and the pattern consists of eight-petaled roses placed closely together. The original mittens, which must have been knitted with exceptionally fine yarn, had five pattern repeats on each side, which translates to 112 stitches around.

The exact same pattern is used on a pair of wrist warmers from Bentgården in Feragen. They were knitted with green and black handspun yarn but had seven repeats around. I decided to reduce the repeats to six.

It seems like it was common to fold up the cuffs on men's mittens and gloves in the district. I decided to knit long single-color cuffs—a standard feature of traditional women's mittens.

Extra fine yarn was used for these mittens. If you want to copy them, you'll need 112 stitches on the needles. Of course, the needles must be correspondingly small!

Thumb

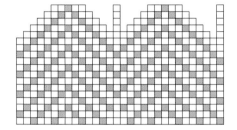

☐ Red-Violet—knit
▨ Gray—knit

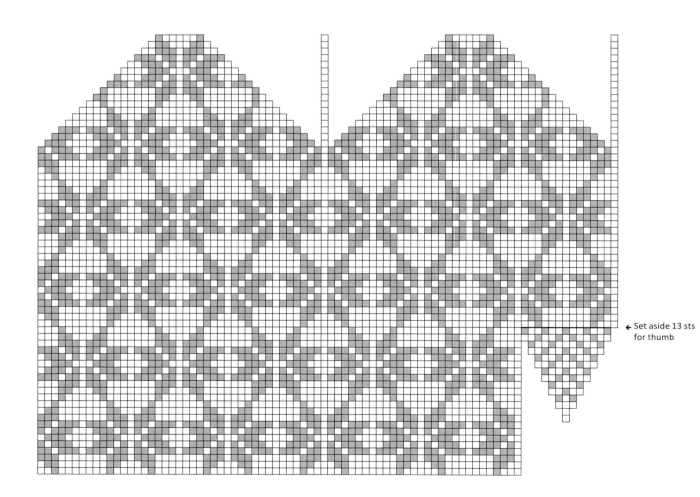

← Set aside 13 sts for thumb

154

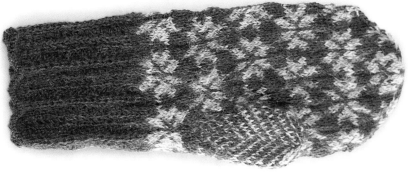

INSTRUCTIONS

Sizes: Women's (Men's)

MATERIALS
Yarn:
CYCA #1 (fingering), Symre from Telespinn (80% Norwegian mohair, 20% Norwegian lamb's wool, 330 yd/302 m / 100 g)

Yarn Amounts
Red-Violet S277: 50 (100) g
Light Gray S010: 50 (100) g

Needles: U.S. size 0 (1.5) / 2 (2.5) mm, set of 5 dpn

Gauge: 34 (31) sts = 4 in / 10 cm.
Adjust needle size to obtain correct gauge if necessary.

Right Mitten
With Red-Violet, CO 77 sts. Divide sts over 4 dpn and join to work in the round. Work in "corrugated" cuff as follows:
Rnd 1: (P1, k10) around.
Rnd 2: *P1, k2tog, k2, yo, k2, yo, k2, k2tog tbl*; rep * to * around.
Rep Rnds 1-2 until cuff measures 4 (3¼) in / 10 (8) cm.

On the next rnd, dec evenly spaced around to 70 sts. Continue in charted pattern.

Increase for the thumb gusset as shown. At the dark line, set aside 13 sts for the thumb (see page 15 for details). Continue following the chart. Shape top as shown on chart. (see page 13 for details). Cut yarn and draw end through rem sts; tighten.

Thumb
Pick up and knit 15 + 15 sts = 30 sts total around thumbhole. Divide sts onto 4 dpn and work in pattern as shown on thumb chart. Cut yarn and draw end through rem sts; tighten.

Left Mitten
Work mirror-image following the chart.

Finishing
Weave in all ends neatly on WS. For a nice wavy edge to the cuff, pin out each point. Spray the mittens with water until thoroughly dampened and leave to dry for at least 24 hours. The cuff on the men's version is folded double.

Striped Mittens

In the early 1800s, Ola Hansson (1760-1843) painted a suitor scene on a round bentwood box from Nes in Telemark. On the lid, we see the suitor to the left. The spokesman is in the middle, and the young woman's father is on the right side. The spokesman—or the best man, as he is sometimes called—has a glass in his hand and is about to raise a toast because the proposal has been accepted. The suitor at the side has a pair of mittens in his hands. They would presumably have been knitted by the young woman, and by giving him the mittens, she signaled that she was willing to marry him.

It was common to put a great deal of work into such engagement gifts. The mittens would be examined and judged by the bride's new family, so she had to make the most of the opportunity to demonstrate how skilled she was.

The family circle often decided who should marry whom. Families and family relations were much more important in those days than they are now. When marriage was on the table, families considered conditions and position, finances and property, and sometimes even politics.

Alf Prøysen has, in a humorous way, portrayed a girl who tried to knit her beloved a sweater. She comes to show him the garment before it is finished and it turns out that wasn't an especially good idea:

So listen, all you girls, girls far and near
Never mention that you knit for the good boy you love
But do as wise women in our high north:
Slip the sweater over his head before a word is said!

I like two-color ribbing, and have experimented with various alternatives. For these mittens, the fine stripes from the beginning continue all the way to the top. The combination of two knit stitches and one purl helps make the mittens fit well on the hands.

Thumb

- ☐ Pink—knit
- ▨ Red—knit
- v Red—purl
- • Inc 1 st knitwise with Pink
- ✕ Inc 1 st purlwise with Red

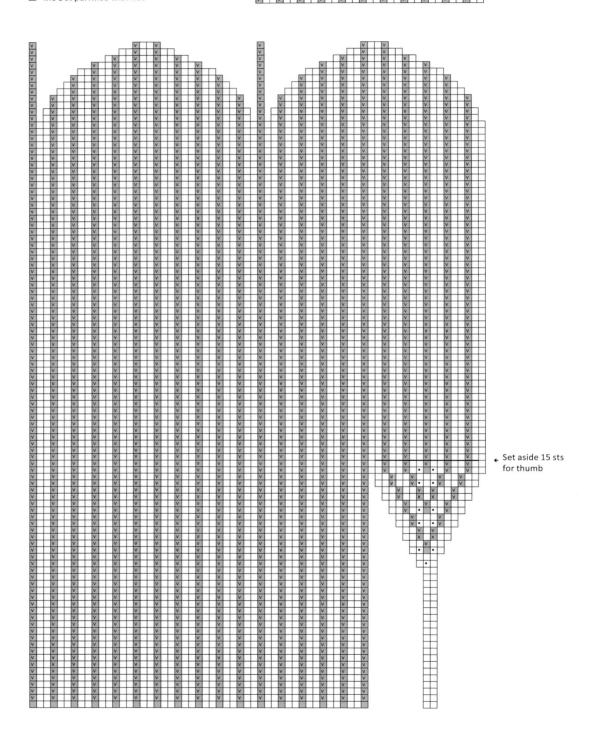

← Set aside 15 sts for thumb

INSTRUCTIONS

Sizes: Women's (Men's)

MATERIALS
Yarn:
CYCA #1 (fingering), Babyull from Dale (100% Merino wool, 180 yd/165 m / 50 g), Red 4018: 50 (100) g
CYCA #2 (sport), Arroyo from Malabrigo (100% Merino wool, 335 yd/306 m / 100 g), English Rose 057: 50 (100) g

Needles: U.S. size 1.5 (2.5) / 2.5 (3) mm, set of 5 dpn

Gauge: 30 (27) sts = 4 in / 10 cm. Adjust needle size to obtain correct gauge if necessary.

Right Mitten
With Pink, CO 51 sts. Divide sts over 4 dpn and join to work in the round. Work in St st for ¾ in / 2 cm and then make an eyelet fold-line: (k2tog, yo) around. Continue, following the chart.

Increase for the thumb gusset as shown. At the dark line, set aside 15 sts for the thumb (see page 15 for details). Continue following the chart. Shape top as shown on chart (see page 13 for details). Cut yarn and draw end through rem sts; tighten.

Thumb
Pick up and knit 17 + 16 sts = 33 sts total around thumbhole. Divide sts onto 4 dpn and work in pattern as shown on thumb chart. Cut yarn and draw end through rem sts; tighten.

Left Mitten
Work mirror-image following the chart.

Finishing
Weave in all ends neatly on WS. Fold cuff at eyelet round and loosely sew down edge on WS. Gently steam press under a damp pressing cloth to block.

Mittens from Lierne

The Sverresborg Trøndelag Folk Museum was given this pair of mittens, knitted with black and white wool, from someone who received them in 1919. The mittens originally had the same pattern all around, but the inside of the palm seems to have gotten so worn that it was reknitted with a different yarn and pattern. I've reconstructed the original patterning.

You might recognize the black and white geometric pattern from Scottish mittens—the so-called Sanquhar gloves from the town of the same name.

Beginning in the Middle Ages, Sanquhar developed to become one of Scotland's most important centers of wool marketing. National wool prices were determined at the wool market in July, and characteristic two-color knitted products were also traded here. According to a travel description from the early 1700s, mittens from here were cheaper and better than those one could find in England. In both the eighteenth and nineteenth centuries, knitting was an important home industry in the region. Many poor families could supplement their income by knitting gloves and stockings. Sanquhar has many parallels to Trøndelag.

The original pair has a button on one mitten and a button loop on the other.

Mittens were practical accessories that quickly became worn and full of holes, especially on the inside of the thumb and palm. When they could no longer be patched, parts of them were re-knitted—as here—and given new life.

Thumb

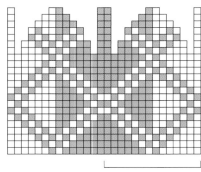

Front of thumb

☐ Red—knit
☐ Pink—knit

← Set aside 12 sts for thumb

INSTRUCTIONS

Sizes: Women's (Men's)

MATERIALS
Yarn:
CYCA #1 (fingering), Gammelserie from Rauma (100% wool, 175 yd/160 m / 50 g), Red 424: 50 (100) g
CYCA #1 (fingering), Babyull from Dale (100% Merino wool, 180 yd/165 m / 50 g), Pink 4516: 50 (100) g

Needles: U.S. sizes 0 and 1.5 (1.5 and 2.5) / 2 and 2.5 (2.5 and 3) mm, set of 5 dpn

Gauge: 28 (25) sts = 4 in / 10 cm.
Adjust needle sizes to obtain correct gauge if necessary.

Right Mitten
With Red and smaller needles, CO 72 sts. Divide sts over 4 dpn and join to work in the round. Work around in k2, p1 ribbing for 2¾ in (7 cm). Change to larger size dpn and St st. Continue, following the chart. At the dark line, set aside 12 sts for the thumb (see page 15 for details). Continue, following the chart. Shape top as shown (see page 13 for details). Cut yarn and draw end through rem sts; tighten.

Thumb
Pick up and knit 14 + 14 sts = 28 sts total around thumbhole. Divide sts onto 4 dpn and work in pattern as shown on thumb chart. Cut yarn and draw end through rem sts; tighten.

Left Mitten
Work mirror-image following the chart.

Finishing
Weave in all ends neatly on WS. Gently steam press under a damp pressing cloth to block.

Fishermen's Mittens from Lofoten

All along the coast, from Hvaler in the south to Kirkenes in the north, women have spun yarn and knitted mittens for their husbands and sons who went to sea. Four or five pairs of mittens were needed for Lofoten fishing. The mittens had somewhat different shapes but all were knitted with wool yarn from villsau or Trønder sheep and felted so they'd be strong and warm. Wool was especially well-suited for the heavy and cold work at sea. These examples are from Vestvågøy.

These days, we add nylon to garments that need to be hardwearing. For fishermen's mittens, it wasn't uncommon to blend wool with hair collected from women's hairbrushes; horse tail hair or goat hair was also used sometimes. These mittens did not felt as much as those made of pure wool, but they were noticeably stronger.

On the east side of the Oslo fjord, hair mittens were common. Some blended hair with wool, but others laid the hair directly into the knitted garment. The work took a long time—and left a lot of strands on the floor!

Fishermen's mittens could be quite large, much wider than other mittens. They were held in place with a cord tied around the wrist. There were distinct mittens for longlining and gillnetting use, as well as for slaughtering caught fish. For rowing, there was another type of mitten. After 1850, there were many places, especially north of Lofoten, where it was common to wear mittens with two thumbs. That way, the mittens could be worn on either hand and would wear out evenly.

Every evening, when the fishermen came in with the catch, the mittens were rinsed and washed out in the sea, slapped against a rock, and hung up in the boathouse or boat. If there was snow, the men could trample them clean. Initials were often embroidered in with red thread so each man could distinguish his mittens from everyone else's. The next morning, the mittens would have to be thawed, which was done by dipping them in the sea. They could also dry out under the men's backsides as they rowed. As soon as the mittens warmed up, they were put on again.

After a while, the mittens would shrink and harden; they also got worn out, so new ones had to be made each year.

These two men are taking a break from fishing in the Lofoten archipelago to have their photo taken. Both are wearing work clothes, including well-felted wool mittens. The photo was taken in Reine, outside Lofoten (Nordland), in about 1910.

INSTRUCTIONS

Sizes: Men's

MATERIALS

Yarn:
CYCA #4 (Aran), 2-ply Villsau from Selbu Spinneri (100% wool, 153 yd/140 m / 100 g), Natural Gray: 100 g

Needles: U.S. sizes 6 / 4 mm, set of 5 dpn

Gauge: 17 sts before felting = 4 in / 10 cm. Adjust needle size to obtain correct gauge if necessary.

Right Mitten
CO 48 sts and knit back and forth in garter st until there are 4 ridges (= 8 rows). Divide sts evenly over 4 dpn (= 12 sts per needle) and join to work in the round. Work 11 rnds in St st. Purl 1 rnd, knit 1 rnd, purl 1 rnd. Continue in St st, and, on the 1st rnd, increase as follows: *K1, M1, knit to end of needle; knit across next needle until 1 st rem, M1, k1*. Rep * to * on last 2 needles. Inc the same way on every 4th rnd 2 more times = 60 sts. When mitten is 6 in / 15 cm long, 2 sts in from right side of palm, set aside 10 sts for thumb (see page 15 for details). Divide sts on dpn so there are 15 sts on each needle.

Continue in St st until mitten is 9¾-11¾ in / 25-30 cm long and then shape top as follows:
Rnd 1: *K2, sl 1, pass the 2nd st over the 3rd st. Knit until 4 sts rem on Needle 2. K2tog, k2*. Rep * to * over next two needles.
Rnd 2: Knit.
Work Rnds 1-2 4 times and then dec on every rnd until 2 sts rem on each needle. Cut yarn and draw end through rem sts; tighten.

Thumb
Pick up and knit 12 + 12 sts = 24 sts total around thumbhole. Divide sts onto 4 dpn and work around in St st until thumb is 2½ in / 6 cm long. Shape tip as follows:
Rnd 1: *K2, sl 1, pass the 2nd st over the 3rd st. Knit until 3 sts rem on Needle 2. K2tog, k1*. Rep * to * over next two needles.
Rnd 2: Knit.
Work Rnds 1-2 2 times and then dec on every rnd until 2 sts rem on each needle. Cut yarn and draw end through rem sts; tighten.

Left Mitten
Work as for right mitten but place the thumb 2 sts in from the left side of palm.

Cords
For each mitten, cut 3 strands of yarn each 35½ in / 90 cm long. Thread through side opposite the thumb, between the 2 ridges at wrist so they are doubled = 6 strands each 17¾ / 45 cm long. Braid the strands in pairs. Finish each with a little tassel.

Felting
We recommend that you felt the mittens by hand so the yarn will felt only a little. Use a felting or washing board, a basin of lukewarm water, and neutral soap (for example, Ivory soap flakes).

If you want shorter mittens, arrange them lengthwise on the board and rub. If you want narrower mittens, place them horizontally on the board and rub. Continue rubbing until the mittens are the right size. Rinse out the soap, shape the mittens, and lay flat until dry.

Nina's Children's Mittens

Norway has about a million winter-fed sheep, who produce an average of 1.5 lambs each. In the summers, the total count is about 2.5 million animals, and they produce about 12.12 million pounds / 5.5 million kilos of wool.

There are nine sheep breeds we can call Norwegian: Dalasau, rygjasau, steigar, spælsau (spelsau), and Gammelnorsk (old Norwegian) sheep, also called villsau (wild sheep). In addition, there are the endangered gray Trøndersau, blæset sheep and fuglestadbrogete sheep.

About one quarter of the sheep in Norway are spælsau. Their wool is characterized by a long and lustrous outer coat and a fine undercoat. The gammelnorsk spælsau are descended from the oldest Norwegian sheep. Gammelnorsk sheep are spread out along the coast and ever more farmers are working with this sheep breed.

What makes a good mitten? Obviously it has to be warm—but it also has to be easy to put on and it has to fit well. Inspired by the shape of various fishermen's mittens, I designed this children's mitten to fulfill these needs.

Sheep are normally clipped two times a year. This photo is most likely of a mother and daughter carefully clipping the animals. Every fiber was meticulously cared for. "The sheep shearing" was taken by Knud Knudsen at Tokheim near Odda in 1872.

INSTRUCTIONS

Sizes: 8 (10, 12) years

MATERIALS
Yarn:
CYCA #5 (bulky), PT3 from Rauma (100% wool, 91 yd/83 m / 50 g), Green 7045: 50 (50, 50) g

Needles: U.S. size 6 (7, 8) / 4 (4.5, 5) mm, set of 5 dpn

Gauge: 19 (18, 17) sts = 4 in / 10 cm. Adjust needle size to obtain correct gauge if necessary.

Right Mitten
CO 40 sts. Working back and forth, knit 4 rows (= 2 ridges). Divide sts evenly over 4 dpn and join to work in the round = 10 sts per needle. Knit 2 rnds and then shape cuff as follows:
Rnd 1: *Ssk at beg of Needle 1, knit until 2 sts rem on Needle 2, and k2tog at end of Needle 2*; rep * to * on Needles 3 and 4.
Rnd 2: Knit.
Work Rnds 1-2 3 times = 28 sts rem.

Knit 2 rnds.

Inc rnds:
Rnd 1: *M1 at beg of Needle 1, knit to end of Needle 2 and M1 at end of Needle 2*; rep * to * on Needles 3 and 4.
Rnd 2: Knit.
Work Rnds 1-2 two times = 36 sts.

Set aside 6 sts for thumb at right side of palm (see page 15 for details). Continue in St st until mitten measures 6 (6¼, 6¾) in / 15 (16, 17) cm long.

Now shape top as follows:
Rnd 1: Ssk at beginning of Needle 1, knit to last 2 sts of Needle 2, and k2tog at end of Needle 2. Knit to end of rnd.
Rnd 2: Knit.
Rnd 3: Knit across Needles 1 and 2. Ssk at beginning of Needle 3, knit to last 2 sts on Needle 4, and k2tog at end of Needle 4.
Rnd 4: Knit.
Work Rnds 1-4 2 times and then decrease at each side of hand on every rnd until 1 st rem on each needle. Cut yarn and draw end through rem sts; tighten.

Thumb
Pick up and knit 8 + 8 sts = total of 16 sts (see page 15). Divide sts over 4 dpn and work around in St st until thumb is 1½ (1¾, 2) in / 4, (4.5, 5) cm long. Ssk at beginning of Needles 1 and 3 and k2tog at end of Needles 2 and 4 until 1 st rem on each needle. Cut yarn and draw end through rem sts; tighten.

Left Mitten
Work as for right mitten but place thumb on left side of palm.

Finishing
Seam the garter st edge on each mitten at the side. Weave in all ends neatly on WS. Gently steam press under a damp pressing cloth to block.

Mittens from Kåfjord

Between 1920 and 1950, Anna Grostøl (1894-1962) traveled around Norway to collect examples of handicrafts and handmade techniques. She recorded, photographed, and filmed. Sami Grene braid weaving in Kåfjord especially interested her, but her collection also has a photo of a pair of mittens from the same place: "Olderdalen, Kåfjord, Troms, 1947."

The mittens were knitted using an intarsia-style twisting technique that's typical for Sami mittens. The single-color sections are worked in the round on double-pointed needles, with the pattern sections worked back and forth. Yarn was expensive, so the pattern yarn didn't go all the way around but was twisted around the background color before knitting back.

Agnes Joramo (born in 1895), told Anna Grostøl in 1947 that she sold mittens from Manndalen at the market in Bossekop. The market was held from the end of November until the last days of February. "I had mittens and braids with me. I could sell 2,000 pairs of mittens every time. We bought it all up here in Manndalen."

Randi Andersen, wife of a fisherman and farmer, was born in Olderdalen in 1924, and related that "for years, mittens were knitted in about one-fourth of the houses in Olderdalen for the Skibotten market." The market took place on 12 November and the braids and mittens were bestsellers. The mittens weren't very large because "they were mittens to wear under leather mittens."

Thumb

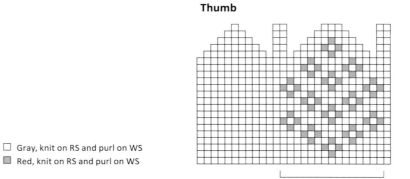

□ Gray, knit on RS and purl on WS
▨ Red, knit on RS and purl on WS

Front of thumb

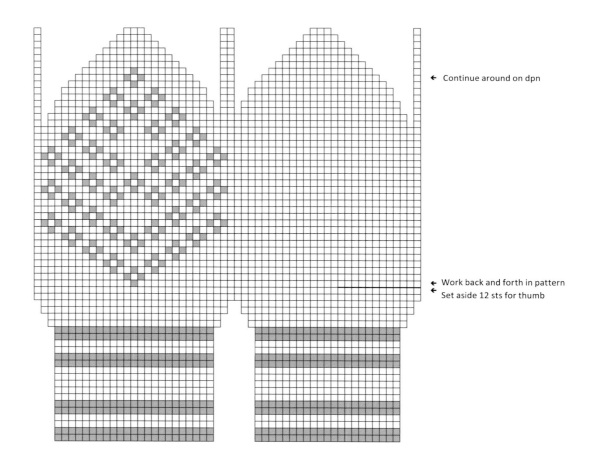

← Continue around on dpn

← Work back and forth in pattern
← Set aside 12 sts for thumb

INSTRUCTIONS

Sizes: Women's (Men's)

MATERIALS
Yarn:
CYCA #2 (sport), 2-ply Trøndersau from Selbu Spinneri (100% wool, 345 yd/315 m / 100 g) OR Ask (Hifa 2) from Hillesvåg Ullvare-fabrikk.

Yarn Amounts:
Light Gray: 50 (100) g
Red: 50 (100) g

Needles: U.S. sizes 2.5 (4) / 3 (3.5) mm, set of 5 dpn; circular for ease of working back and forth

Gauge: 22 (19) sts = 4 in / 10 cm.
Adjust needle size to obtain correct gauge if necessary.

Right Mitten
With Gray, CO 44 sts. Divide sts over 4 dpn and join to work in the round. Work around in k2, p2 ribbing for 1½ in (4 cm). Add Red and continue in St st following the chart.

Continue, following the chart. At the dark line, set aside 12 sts for the thumb (see page 15 for details). When you reach the patterning on the front of the mitten, work intarsia back and forth on a circular. After completing pattern, return to dpn and knitting in the round. Shape top as shown (see page 13 for details). Cut yarn and draw end through rem sts; tighten.

Thumb
Pick up and knit 14 + 14 sts = 28 sts total around thumbhole. Work back and forth on circular following the charted thumb pattern. Cut yarn and draw end through rem sts; tighten.

Left Mitten
Work mirror-image following the chart.

Finishing
Seam the sides of hand and thumb. Weave in all ends neatly on WS. Gently steam press under a damp pressing cloth to block.

Mittens from Kautokeino

Between 1838 and 1840, the French scientific research expedition "Recherche" visited Iceland, the Faroe Islands, and Norway. As well as other places, they visited Bossekop and Kautokeino. Among the items carried by the expedition, we find a color lithograph by August Mayer which shows "the inside of a farmer's cabin in Finnmark." Several of those in the cabin are wearing mittens with panels around the wrist and simple patterns on the back of the hand. This indicates that, by that time, the Sami were already familiar with the technique of knitting with several colors.

Concerning mittens from Kautokeino, Berit Hætta writes that after sheep holding began, spinning, weaving, and knitting were common amongst the settled Sami. "In Kautokeino, the knitted mitten has had a very interesting development from the end of the 19th century up until now. After they learned how to dye yarn or could buy yarn in many colors, the mittens were knitted with colorful, self-designed patterns which embellished the entire mitten. The background color was preferably white, with red, blue, and green as common pattern colors. Following the customs and usage in Kautokeino, the patterns were individually designed so that no two pairs of mittens were alike. It was also common to knit in the 'name signs' (runes) of those who owned the mittens on the thumb."

These mittens were made much like a pair sold at Husfliden (a handcrafts shop) in Kautokeino in the 1950s.

If you study the pictured mittens closely, you'll notice the two mittens to the right are not alike. The mitten underneath is the one which has been reconstructed.

Thumb

Braided Cord

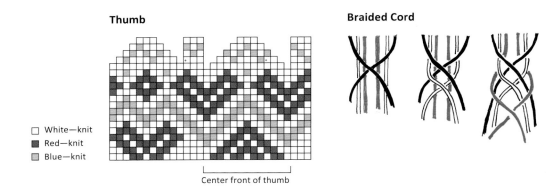

Center front of thumb

☐ White—knit
■ Red—knit
▨ Blue—knit

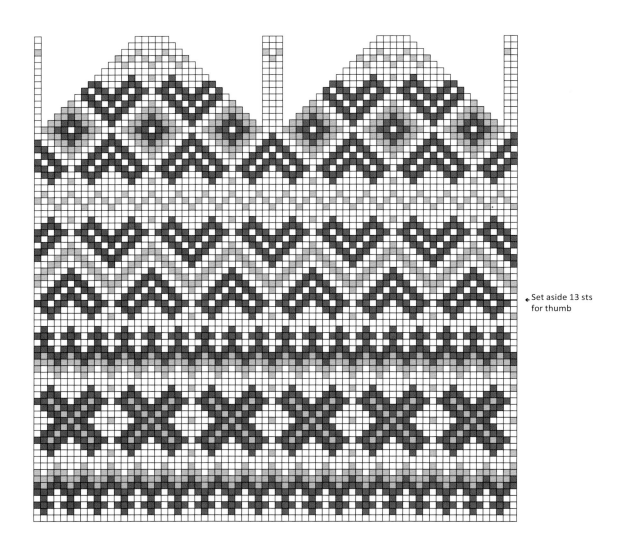

← Set aside 13 sts
for thumb

178

INSTRUCTIONS

Sizes: Women's (Men's)

MATERIALS
Yarn:
CYCA #2 (sport), PT2 from Rauma (100% wool, 180 yd/165 m / 50 g)

Yarn Amounts
Red 88: 50 (100 g)
Blue 36: 50 (100) g
White 00: 50 (100) g

Needles: U.S. size 1.5 (2.5) / 2.5 (3) mm: straights and set of 5 dpn

Gauge: 29 (26) sts = 4 in / 10 cm.
Adjust needle size to obtain correct gauge if necessary.

Right Mitten
With Red around thumb and White over index finger, use long-tail method to CO 72 sts. Divide sts evenly over 4 dpn and join to work in the round. Work 1 rnd two-end purl braid (see page 14) with Red and White. Work another rnd of purl braid with Red and Blue.

Continue, following the chart. At the dark line, set aside 13 sts for the thumb (see page 15 for details). Shape top as shown (see page 13 for details). Cut yarn and draw end through rem sts; tighten.

Thumb
Pick up and knit 15 + 15 sts = 30 sts total around thumbhole. Divide sts onto 4 dpn and work following the thumb chart. Cut yarn and draw end through rem sts; tighten.

Left Mitten
Work mirror-image following the chart.

Finishing
Weave in all ends neatly on WS. Gently steam press under a damp pressing cloth to block.

Braided Cords:
Measure two strands of each color, about 35½ in / 90 cm long each. Thread through edge of mitten, opposite thumb, so strands are doubled = 12 strands each about 17¾ / 45 cm long. Group the strands so you have 2 Red, 2 White, and 2 Blue. Braid as shown in the drawing on page 178.

Tassels:
Wind the yarn 7-8 times around four fingers held together or until tassel is thick enough. Cut a strand to wrap 2-3 times around near the top of the tassel and fasten off securely (the end can be slid under the wraps and down into the tassel. Cut bottom loops open; attach tassel to cord.

American Mittens

Access to wool yarn and ready-made knitted garments was limited in America. This little ad in the Fædrelandsvennen (Friends of the Fatherland) is witness to that:

"Immigrants traveling to America, should, before they travel, stock up on knitted goods at my warehouse, because they will cost two to four times more over there. Kristiansand's Knitting Factory, Jacob Lauridsen."

The starting point for this mitten pattern was a little child's mitten in the Vesterheim Museum collection, at the national Norwegian-American Museum in Decorah, Iowa. These are from about 1900. The museum has a number of mittens knitted in the Norwegian tradition. Even though immigrants couldn't bring very much with them to America on the trip over the ocean, they carried knowledge and traditions along with their baggage. Besides, it was just as cold in the northern U.S. as in Norway!

Ole Paulson brought mittens along as a little gift from Norway when he visited his relative, Ingeborg Haldorsdatter Jacobson, around the turn of the last century. Ingeborg was the daughter of Haldor and Siri Eidem from Selbu. She lived with her husband, Knut, and daughter, Mathea, who received these mittens.

Thumb

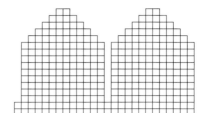

☐ White—knit
▨ Pink—knit
ⱱ White—purl
ⱱ Pink—purl

Chart 2

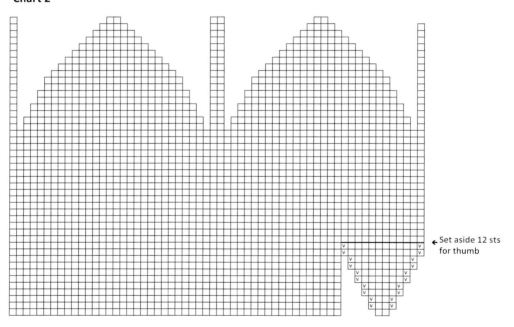

← Set aside 12 sts for thumb

Chart 1

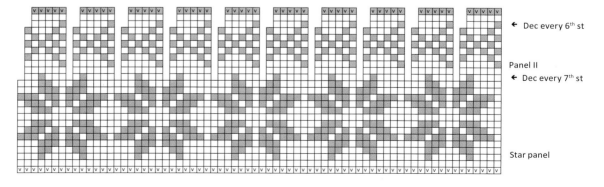

← Dec every 6th st

Panel II
← Dec every 7th st

Star panel

INSTRUCTIONS

Sizes: 4 (6) years

MATERIALS
Yarn:
CYCA #1 (fingering), Lanett Babyull Super-wash from Sandnes Garn (100% wool, 191 yd/175 m / 50 g), White 1001: 50 (50) g
CYCA #1 (fingering), Babyull from Dale (100% Merino wool, 180 yd/165 m / 50 g), Pink 4516: 50 (50) g

Needles: U.S. size 0 (1.5) / 2 (2.5) mm: straights and set of 5 dpn

Gauge: 34 (32) sts = 4 in / 10 cm. Adjust needle size to obtain correct gauge if necessary.

Right Mitten
With Pink, CO 70 sts. Divide sts evenly over 4 dpn and join to work in the round. Purl 1 rnd with White as shown on chart and then continue with star panel on Chart 1. On the last rnd of the star panel, dec every 7th st = a total of 10 sts decreased (1 st between each star point and each star = 60 sts rem. On the last rnd of Panel II, dec on every 6th st = 50 sts rem. End Chart 1 by purling 1 rnd with Pink as shown; cut Pink.

With White only, continue to Chart 2. Increase for the thumb gusset as shown. At the dark line, set aside 12 sts for the thumb (see page 15 for details). Shape top as shown (see page 13 for details). Cut yarn and draw end through rem sts; tighten.

Thumb
Pick up and knit 13 + 13 sts = 26 sts total around thumbhole. Divide sts onto 4 dpn and knit 2 rnds. On the next rnd, dec 1 st at each side = 24 sts rem. Continue to end of chart. Cut yarn and draw end through rem sts; tighten.

Left Mitten
Work mirror-image following the chart.

Finishing
Weave in all ends neatly on WS. Gently steam press under a damp pressing cloth to block.

Peacock Mittens

In 1989, I was on a reporting trip to Denmark to write about mohair goats. At the time, the Norwegian authorities were very skeptical about importing cloven-hoofed animals because they might bring in diseases. In addition, the Norwegian sheep and goat association didn't think it would be economically viable to establish mohair production. Three years later, in 1992, the Norwegian Mohair Company was created to import embryos from Denmark and live animals from New Zealand.

Over the past few years, interest in mohair has steadily increased, which isn't a surprise considering how luxurious the fiber is. It's lustrous, warm, soft, moth resistant, anti-static, and it repels dirt.

This pretty blue and green yarn made me think of peacocks, and the pattern was inspired by the fascinating feathers of these elegant birds.

The luxurious fiber from mohair goats has become ever more popular in Norway.

Thumb

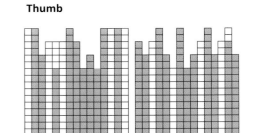

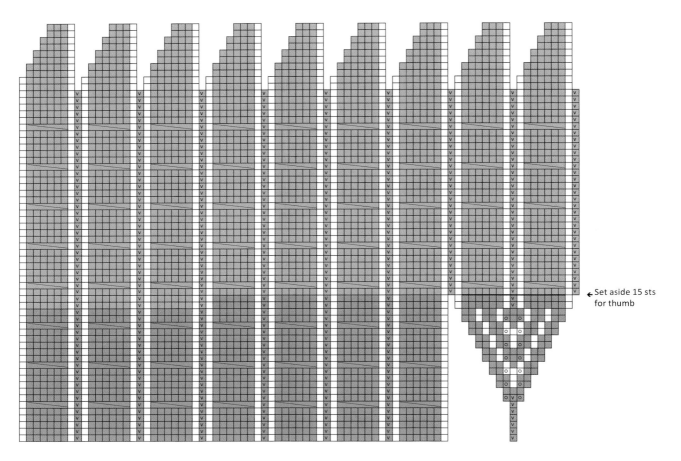

← Set aside 15 sts for thumb

Chart 1

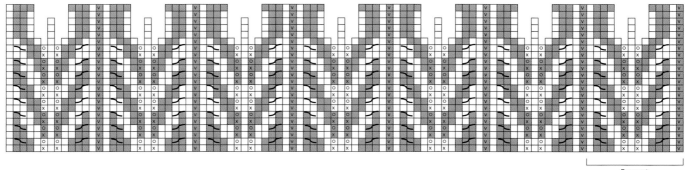

Repeat

186

INSTRUCTIONS

Sizes: Women's (Men's)

MATERIALS
Yarn:
CYCA #2 (sport), Mohair by Canard (65% mohair, 35% Merino wool, 193 yd/176 m / 50 g)

Yarn Amounts
Blue 2002: 50 (100) g
Green 2099: 50 (100) g

Needles: U.S. size 1.5 (2.5) / 2.5 (3) mm, set of 5 dpn; cable needle

Gauge: 34 (31) sts in pattern = 4 in / 10 cm. Adjust needle size to obtain correct gauge if necessary.

Right Mitten
With Green, CO 84 sts. Divide sts over 4 dpn and join to work in the round. Work following Chart 1; the repeat is worked a total of 7 times around. After completing charted rows, 63 sts rem. Continue to Chart 2. Increase for thumb gusset as shown. At the dark line, set aside 15 sts for the thumb (see page 15 for details). Continue following the chart. Shape top as shown on chart (see page 13 for details). Cut yarn and draw end through rem sts; tighten.

Thumb
Pick up and knit 16 + 16 sts = 32 sts total around thumbhole. Divide sts onto 4 dpn and work in pattern as shown on thumb chart. Cut yarn and draw end through rem sts; tighten.

Left Mitten
Work mirror-image following the chart.

Finishing
Weave in all ends neatly on WS. Pin out mittens, pinning out cuffs so that gentle waves follow the pattern. Spray with lukewarm water and leave to dry for at least 24 hours.

YARN RESOURCES

Anzula: www.anzula.com

Artyarns: www.artyarns.com

Blue Sky Fibers: www.blueskyfibers.com

Dale Garn: www.dalegarnnorthamerica.com

Malabrigo: www.malabrigoyarn.com

Sandnes Garn: www.sandnes-garn.com

If you are unable to obtain any of the yarn used in this book, it can be replaced with a yarn of a similar weight and composition. Please note, however, that the finished products may vary slightly from those shown, depending on the yarn used. Try www.yarnsub.com for suggestions.

For more information on selecting or substituting yarn, contact your local yarn shop or an online store; they are familiar with all types of yarns and would be happy to help you. Additionally, the online knitting community at Ravelry.com has forums where you can post questions about specific yarns. Yarns come and go so quickly these days and there are so many beautiful yarns available.

PHOTO CREDITS

ACKNOWLEDGMENTS

A big thank you to everyone who helped with matters both large and small, and who enthusiastically supported me throughout, especially my very patient husband. A special thanks to the staff at museums I visited and those who helped me with research in the collections and archives.
Maihaugen, Lillehammmer Museum
Selbu Township Museum
Setesdal Museum
The Cultural History Collections, University in Bergen
Osterøy Museum
Sunnfjord Museum
Nordfjord Folk Museum
The Heiberg Collections—Sogn Folk Museum
Hallingdal Museum
Norwegian Institute for Folk Dress and Costumes
Thank you also to the Norwegian Non-fiction Writers and Translators Organization and, not least, Cappelen Damm, who had faith in this project.

This book was supported by a grant from the Norwegian Non-fiction Writers and Translators Organization.